I0159212

A i j a M .

THE X-FILES SERIES

X-1 ASIAN PERSUASION

Copyright ©2012 by Aija M. Butler

PAPERBACK FORMAT

Printed in the United States of America

ISBN-13: **978-0615639062**

ISBN-10: 0615639062

Cover Design: Aija M. Butler

Cover Photos: Dreamstime.com

Publisher: AMB Publications

ambpublising@gmail.com

X-FILES SERIES
Asian PERSUASION

Prologue

Chen watched Gun and his guest from afar. She was fixated on Gun's companion. His pearly white smile and deep dimples lured her interests far beyond how deep his pockets may have been. She had money. She was far more interested in the bulge of his pants. She was married to Gun; but their love for one another had long since dissipated. Chen hid secrets so deep; they couldn't be recovered if she were buried with them.

Her horrific childhood…, the death of her parents, not to mention her brothers suicide, or how she was sold to the man she thought truly loved her. Chen once thought she was the lucky one, one who had escaped the true elements of a political marriage.

Chen was always looking for a way out. It wasn't long after the first beating she looked towards freedom. She was tired of Gun's game. She began to develop one of her own.

"Cream and sugar..?" Chen asked Terrence as her almond eyes peeked from under her sheer mask.

"Cream…," Terrence responded loud and clear. He tipped his cup in her direction to offer a Thank you. His eyes never met hers. Chen found that odd about Terrence, she didn't know whether to take his lack of interest as a sign of disrespect, or respect for Gun and his possessions earning him a badge of honor.

Gun himself, liked his girls half dressed with their face covered. He said that no one really cared what a woman looked like. They were more concerned about the package. Chen was his girl but she was often used to entice his prey. She feared Gun, but she feared her desires more. Chen feared that her wants would soon be the death of her.

Meeting Terrence was the best thing that had happened to her. He was Gun's confident, but to her he was her savior.

Mob Figure... "Hurry up, Chen grab all that you can. We have to get out of here."

"Were you followed?" Chen questioned Gun which is something she didn't normally do, but under the circumstances she felt that she had a little le-way in the matter.

Gun paused and eyed Chen to warn her that nothing had changed. She had better do as told or he would leave her to the wolves. Though he knew that wasn't his reality. The money he'd stolen was just that. Stolen goods and if and when the mob found him they would not only take back their possessions they would be sure to kill him in the process.

"Chen, just hurry please no questions just do it. We really don't have the time and I need to know that I can count on you."

Chen rolled her eyes, but not in his direction. She knew better.

Gun was running about their Korean mansion so fiercely trying to grab the duffle bags and load them into the trunk of his suburban. He was saddened that he would have to leave his most prize possessions but the two of them should consider themselves lucky if they could get out of there with their lives.

Gun ducked suddenly as if his cameras surrounding their mansion could see his whereabouts inside the home.

He took one look at the screen and could see the thugs surrounding his home.

"Chen…" he whispered as loud as he could trying desperately to get her attention

Chen was working like a bat out of hell throwing her belongings inside Guns truck. She was serious about her mission. Gun ducked and dodged the large windows of the house trying to hurry and get to Chen before they caught sight of her.

"Chen..," Gun ran to her side in a desperate move to save them both.

"Take off your shoes and get down they are outside. I know their strategy they are going to come in through the master bedroom." Chen looked nervous. She had to go inside one last time to grab her financial information from the lock box just under rug tucked away inside Gun's office. Even he didn't know that she had other means to support herself. He did know of her trust, but nothing as substantial as she the load of cash she held close to her heart.

"Just get in the car I have to grab some paperwork."

"No… let's go!"

GUN, Chen yelled surprised at her own reaction. "Trust me…," Chen whispered calmly regaining her composure a bit frightened at what Gun's possible reaction to her defiance could be.

For the first time in years Gun's eyes welled with tears. He was very afraid that she would get caught in the cross fire. He didn't say a word however…, because he had no choice but to trust her.

"Hurry…," He finally spoke as Chen threw her shoes into the car and snuck back into the home low, calm, and collected like a ninja. Chen made her way back up to the second floor before she knew it. She appeared small and fragile but she was well trained. Only she knew that she wasn't a true opponent for Gun with weapon in hand. She did however consider sparring with him on a regular basis, if only he'd rid himself of his toy's and stand-up to face her like a man.

Gun was a terror. In her right mind she would easily use this chance to flee from his grasp; but she couldn't be sure of how serious his transgression against the mob was. So all she could do was hope for the best. Huffing and puffing in an effort to grab hold to her breath she rolled into Gun's office like a spy. She was playing the part for sure by this time.

Chen's hands were shaking once she spotted the men in ski masks bouncing up the stairs of their home. Chen steadied her hands and quickly unlocked the safe, as if disabling a bomb. She grabbed hold to the petty cash totaling one hundred thousand dollars, along with her papers of American citizenship and other pertinent documents. Chen checked her surroundings once more as she noticed the uncomfortable silence as she tucked the information under her dress. Feeling the hairs on the back of her neck begin to stand she took refuge to be sure the coast was clear by slipping into the storage closet.

Shortly, after Chen could hear the men walking by. They were quiet and in their approach; but she could hear the drawers being thrown open and the books on the shelves knocked to the floor. She couldn't be sure if they were looking for money because of the small areas of concern. What had Gun stolen from these people? The very men he was sworn to protect he betrayed, a play for power she knew her father could never have been a part of.

Meanwhile, Gun was sweating bullets as he waited for Chen to return. His selfish mind wanted so much to drive straight through the garage doors and never look back.

Gun pondered what could be taking Chen so long. Perhaps they weren't going to use weapons at all maybe they were going for a silent kill, a true anguish of torture to leave the best for last. That's what he would do and he was sure that they had an agenda as he had killed with these men many times before.

Gun coached his way back to sanity as he waited for Chen's arrival. He was sure they were going to die. The mob was relentless in their prey and they would leave no stone untouched. Gun hadn't felt a stitch of guilt until now. A new feeling to Gun just moments before his fate was sealed. He was marked for death and he had taken innocent Chen down in the process.

Gun took a deep breath and swallowed hard before deciding to load both his 40 calico and 357. He set one on his lap and the other on the dashboard of his truck. He was going to go in hot if Chen didn't make her way back to the car in the next minute. Gun began his count down breathing heavily and blowing steam, nervous but ready to take on the world.

"30...29...28," Gun continued his count as he jumped down from the truck to stand in front of the exit door preparing to fire his weapon at the slightest movement. He was so nervous and trigger happy. Chen would be lucky to miss a bullet herself.

"27...26...25," Gun shifted his weight and readied himself. Just as he looked down to his feet, Chen burst into the door empty handed with his prize, "*Munetoshi Yuki* sword."

Gun looked up startled and out of his element. If she was an intruder she could have easily killed him with one blow. Gun exhaled as Chen fell into the garage and bolted the door behind her. The sword was a little heavy for her body but she held as though it were a small hand gun.

Gun shook his way back into kill or be killed mode and threw his artillery into the passenger seat of the car as he instructed Chen to get into the backseat. It wasn't over yet, but while the men were inside the main home they needed to make a break for it.

The coast seemed clear, as Gun and Chen studied the cameras inside the garage. Gun thought about opening the door to the garage and simply driving out like normal but he couldn't be sure what was lurking in the trees of his campus. Chen lay down on the floor of the backseat with her hand on a gun and the other on the butt of the sword that glistened against the black leather of the backseat. She was ready as ever and had nothing to lose at the moment. It was all or nothing.

Gun took one deep breath as he instructed auto start to chime in. He grabbed hold of his steering wheel so tight his yellow skin paled to a snow white. Inhaling as deep as his chest would allow he put his foot on the gas and sped off driving straight through the garage doors and down the pathway to the main streets of Korea. If they were followed he didn't pay any attention. He was so fixated at the road he didn't care to look back.

It was a grueling two hour drive from Pyongyang North Korea, to Seoul South Korea where they felt safe to board a plane. The flight was nearly thirteen hours.

Gun was so nervous his assassin made the plane ride with him he didn't sleep a wink. With Terrence present he could rest assure his safety; but he was a few hours behind them tying up loose ends.

Terrence, "The Terror," the gang often called him. He was a hot head but calculated in his deliverance of vengeance. Terrence was Guns right hand man a secret he kept from Chen for a number of reasons. He was the one left with blood on his hands the fall guy, so to speak. To Gun, Terrence was his best friend when in his presence but he used him in any and every way possible. He truly needed Terrence; he trusted Terrence with his life but never his women. Only now he would be left with no choice. He was all he had left aside from Chen, and in America she would be sure to test the waters and her new found liberation.

Settling...

Chen quickly fixed breakfast for Gun. She was anxious to get rid of him that morning. Her eyes were still swollen from the beating he had given her for looking at one of his business partners. Her attention lingered about a second too long, and Gun was sure to show her who was boss in the presence of his partners. She begged for help with her eyes but sympathy wasn't granted from him or his thug of a friend. He stood waiting for Gun to grow tired of his play and then asked him if he wanted to share a cigar.

Chen pondered her escape. She was so tired of living under Gun she would rather pay him to let her go. He remained oblivious to her true worth. She knew that is what saved her from an early death. It was cheaper to keep her alive. He was lonely and paranoid. He wouldn't set foot outside until his driver was parked out front or Terrence was on duty. The threats were overwhelming. Gun didn't know who to trust.

Chen smiled slightly as she thought of committing his murder. Lately she had become infatuated with getting to the bottom of her father's untimely death. She was certain it was an inside job and he was falsely accused of betraying the mob. She believed whole and in part that he was framed, and over the last few months Gun had become her number one suspect.

Her curiosity began to peak in the direction of Gun, because when she asked to talk about the matter he became instantly furious. The fact that he was irritated of her questioning him wasn't what set her off. It was his blatant disgust when her Father's name was mentioned. A man Gun claimed to love and wish to immolate. Chen soon became sick to her stomach at the thought of possibly sleeping with the enemy.

Gun finished about a third of his breakfast before wiping his mouth and throwing his napkin into his plate.

"All ready to go babe." Chen urged Gun towards the exit as sincere as she could possibly muster without stirring up a bunch of questions. Since their escape from Korea, Gun was paranoid as ever. Even with Terrence on staff he didn't trust most of his new crew. He was in constant research about the past and present of his men. Chen thought he may have been going crazy and encouraged him time and time again to see someone about his issues; but Gun didn't trust anyone. He presumed the meds would be prescribed in an effort to kill him.

Chen helped Gun situate his holster and blazer before planting a kiss on his cheek. She tried her best to rub the tension from his shoulders as he looked deep into her eyes. It was his way of weeding out the demons that lurked in the confines of a woman's mind.

"Just in case you are planning to leave me, or planning to deceive me, I want you to know that you will be nothing without me, and if for some reason I fall prey to your temptress ways I will haunt you; and if I survive...I will kill you."

Chen took a deep breath but her eyes never wavered from his. The tears that stung her retinas were locked and froze as if ice as her heart had turned cold to Gun's threats. Chen simply smiled and handed Gun his nickel plated nine millimeter one of her favorite companions and waved good-bye.

Once Chen could see Gun's car pull out of the gates of their new home, Chen hurriedly ran to the upstairs bedroom to check out what Gun had stashed in his safe. A hidden treasure Gun was sure Chen had little if any knowledge of.

Chen swore it would be the death of him. Hoarding his riches inside the home he couldn't watch his back at all times. Gun stated that he didn't trust American banks. Gun's most recent activity showed signs of complete loss of control, he was on edge and skeptical even, about the meals Chen prepared for dinner.

Moving to a new location meant he would have to start over. Learn the game and the streets. The Korean mob was ruthless in their hunt for Gun. They barely made it out alive. Chen knew that if it weren't for her blood line, she and Gun would have been thrown into the river in pieces. Gum however would never admit that it was his woman that saved his ass.

Chen had the clout to get them set-up in Los Angeles. What he didn't know was that Chen's father not only set-up a trust for her in Korea, he set-up one for her in the states as well. Apparently, he thought more of her than he ever admitted. This notion warmed her heart. She could be someone else if only she could loosen the restraints Gun had on her. His threats to kill her if she tried to flee were getting redundant and were playing out fast.

Chen's hope was to uncover the mystery behind Gun's hate for her father in the confines of that box. He was always so secretive but as of late his secrets were now a mystery to her as well. The only thing she could ever count on from Gun in the past was the honest and often harsh truth. Only now, it was beyond her wildest dreams to find peace with Gun and his riddled mind. Chen paused for a moment as she pulled the box from buried deep inside the closet. She could have sworn she heard the front door open and close. As a precaution she was always carrying. She didn't want to get caught without protection. She had heard some things about Los Angeles that left a sense of fear and uncertainty about her spirits.

Not that her life in Korea was much different. Except she lived away from the dirt, at least until Gun decided to bite the hand of the men who fed him.

The truth about the mob was just like any other gang. There are ranks, and quite honestly the head honcho isn't the one doing the dirt, it's the flock. They were all looking for a spot on the team. Chen often warned Gun that he wasn't her father's only confidant. He had plenty of followers that seemed to love and respect him, all the more reason to seek out protection from the outside. Many would argue that this is the reason behind the death of Chen's father. They felt as though he was a trader for hiring outside the family.

Being deemed as a trader wasn't his concern however. He never trusted family. "A Family is never satisfied, no matter what you do for them," Mr. Chang often stated and Chen believed him.

Her mother was selfish and a gold digger on the under. She died four years prior to her father's murder, which Chen secretly reveled in. She knew her mother was waiting the poor guy out. Her brother committed suicide shortly after their mother's death. For three years it was just Chen, her father, and Gun. A man she was arranged to marry but also her sweetheart. She glowed and drifted on a cloud in her youth. Nineteen and married to the love of her life was simply unheard of in her part of the world. Marriages were political a form of business, and having a son took precedence to a girl any day.

Chen continued meddling through Gun's private property once she could dismiss the sounds she heard lurking about her abode. Her stomach was filled with anxiety. She couldn't be sure of what he was hiding but she feared the worst. If Gun had, had anything to do with her father's death she would be devastated.

Chen rummaged through the contents of the box in search of something tangible that she could pin on Gun. She noticed that he had two sealed envelopes that read. "P.1 and P.2," Chen was puzzled but she didn't have time to pry the mail open without the materials to reseal it so she quickly put the envelopes back into place and continued in search for clues.

Chen was on all fours trying to piece together the receipts she found among the jewelry and rolls of money. The money wasn't the issue at all. She had been around riches her entire life. Money didn't impress her. It was what her affiliates did with the money that infatuated her. Chen was very much into investing. She was excited about how one dollar could be multiplied into millions. She was just the opposite of her mother. Her mother enjoyed spending, while she enjoyed accumulating.

Chen fumbled amongst the jewelry until she noticed something familiar. She was certain it was her fathers. She would never forget it. It was his necklace her and her brother pitched in and bought him when they were in grade school.

Chen slowly uncovered the necklace and brought it up to the light. The gold on the cross was still intact but she could see some flakes on it just barely. It looked as though it had been cleaned but not thoroughly. As Chen held the corner of the cross up to the light she could clearly see small specks of blood. Her heart sank and the tears blurred her vision as she searched for other incriminating evidence.

Perhaps Gun had kept the necklace to remind him of her father. Or perhaps it was just another souvenir from one of his kills.

Caught red handed...

"Find what you were looking for?" Terrence stood just in front of Gun's cherry desk with his arms folded. He wore his slacks just high enough to tease the naked eye. Chen's eyes traveled down the front of his pants. He watched and as she paused his muscles jumped startling her back to attention.

Terrence had seemed to have forgotten his shirt in his bathroom; but he wasn't uncomfortable about his inappropriate display. Chen was taken back by his forwardness and half naked body that her hands were wet and she was hot under the collar. Chen scurried about the floor trying to put the contents of Gun's treasures back into place without too many eyebrows being raised.

"You got some explaining to do." Terrence laughed maniacally with a Spanish accent.

"I...T...Terrence, I was looking for some paperwork Gun needed for the house is all. With everything going on, he has become quite the paranoid freak and whatever I can do to help...," Chen shrugged. "Is what I must in order to keep my sanity...," Chen rambled on looking about the room still in search for clues. She trusted Terrance, but she couldn't be sure of how loyal to Gun he remained, despite their friendship.

In light of the most recent threats on Gun's life he was taking extra precautions. He was murdering his men, questioning their whereabouts after hours, and she was the temptress in his scheme to reveal the true traitor.

Chen stood looking deep into Terrence's chest as she thought about Gun and his private meetings lingered on.

Terrence was always present but he was usually hush mouth, unless told to participate. It was obvious to Chen that he was a follower. Chen drifted back to the first meeting with Terrence himself. Gun used her even then to make sure his eyes wouldn't waver to possessions that weren't his own.

Terrence wasn't a fool. He knew how beautifully seductive Chen was. He also knew the game. He wasn't willing to play cat and mouse with Gun. He wanted in the family business, despite the pigmentation of his skin.

His father was a close friend of Chen's father and respectfully he was hired to represent Gun and his followers. Terrence saw himself as a separate entity, one that wasn't under Gun but stood off to the side. He made decisions on where and when, though Gun ordered the hits. Terrence felt as if Gun owed him more than anything because he carried out the evil deeds he conjured. Terrence was about actions, so he truly was the one with heart.

Chen knew as much. She too, had grown an attachment to Terrence. The intimacy in Gun and Chen's relationship had long dissipated. She was fearful of Gun, not in love with him. Chen had high hopes for herself in America. She just couldn't bear to leave Gun while he was going through such an ordeal. One that she plotted upon; but most definitely hadn't started. Gun had dug his own grave.

"So can I get by?" Chen's eyes danced playfully around the fullness of Terrence's lips. She was curious of their taste but she threw her thoughts away as soon as they entered her beading brow.

"It's a free country…" Terrence laughed and moved aside just slightly to allow her to pass.

Chen brushed by nervously grazing into him slightly. Their hand's touched and she couldn't be sure of it but she felt his fingers beckon towards hers. It was a gentle gesture but one that sent tingles up her arm and butterflies to flutter in her belly. Chen rushed out of the office nearly sprinting down the hall to her master suite. She needed a cold shower immediately. She was falling fast and she couldn't be sure if Terrence was pulling a move on her as she did so many times before as Gun's bait for his prey. Either way she needed a new venue fast or she would soon find out what Terrence's intentions were…willingly.

Chen jumped into the cold water shivering upon feeling its cool flow. She danced about jiggling as her teeth chattered vowing never to do the cold water again. After her body warmed up to the freezing waters Chen emerged her entire body wetting her pitch black and chocolate hair. Satisfied she had survived her loss of sensibility, Chen turned the water as hot as she could stand it and reached for her milk and honey body wash.

The thick white soap caused her mind to play a number of naughty thoughts as she sensually washed her body with the thick white substance. Chen fell into the doors of the shower, snapping her wavering consciousness back to reality. She was dizzy with her infatuations with Terrence. Embarrassed by her display of idiocy she looked about the bathroom to make sure no one had born witness to her display and quickly rinsed off.

Chen stepped out of the shower and dried off. She took the short walk to her closet in search of a pair of sweats and tee. She needed to get the house cleaned before Gun made it home from his scavenger hunts. Chen put on her blue and white striped panties after she moisturized her body, and went in search for the matching bra. Turning her search to a close empty handed Chen waved a dismissive hand, she decided to go braless. After all she wasn't leaving the home she was just going to do her chores.

Chen's nipples stood at attention underneath her small, "Love Pink," girl shirt. It cut off two full inches above her navel showcasing the smooth contours of her stomach. Her sweats were no better. They hung dangerously low around her pelvic bone giving a slight tease to her spectators.

Chen jogged down the stairs to get a jump on dinner and her chores. Her feet slapped the glossy marble floors as she flipped flopped about her home. She scrubbed and mopped the kitchen floors until the reflection of her feet were present. The music blazed. Alicia Keys was singing one of her favorite tunes, "Unthinkable," Chen's Asian accent had a tad bit of soul to it as she swirled her hips to the beat singing harmoniously into the stick of her broom.

"Great showmanship," Terrence smiled as he presented Chen with a hand clap for her song and dance. He was fully clothed, but dressed in a tank and pajama pants. It appeared he too, was a bit hot under the collar and had to shower away his thoughts of infidelity.

Chen blushed tremendously. As she willed the reddening of her cheeks away it only brightened them. If that wasn't all causing attention to her disposition, her nipples percolated through her tee which created headlines into her most intimate thoughts. Terrence noticed and in that moment he needed to know if she had similar feelings of his own, no matter the consequences.

Chen didn't need a clue, she dropped the meat she fished from the freezer into the sink and jumped right into the fold of Terrence's arms. He caught her as if he had done it thousands of times before and plunged his tongue deep into Chen's hot pink mouth. Their tongues intertwined and when they met the sensation of lust brewing exploded into fireworks of passion.

Chens head fell back as Terrance kissed and licked her done her neck. He suckled and bit her hungrily infatuated with the taste and smell of her skin. He was drunk in love and found himself hoisting Chen up into the air with one arm as if praising his winnings. Chen was lost in her mind for at least thirty seconds counting the times she was likely to climax with such a man.

Terrence let her down slowly as he touched and kissed every inch of her body. She could feel the heat from his loins burning threw his mouth. She could feel the moisture warm her panties. He was making her love come to a head with her clothes on. Chen shook her mind just barely coming to as she realized the nature of their relationship had changed. She was fearful of Gun walking in and felt instant guilt.

Chen stumbled down to her feet and allowed the cool of the floor to turn off the flames. Her feet smoked from the heat and her senses resonated. Forcing herself to do the right thing Chen busied herself walking briskly about the kitchen and into the pantry to find side dishes to accompany her entre'.

Terrence followed her unable to end their rendezvous so quickly. Chen stopped just in front of the pantry's entrance and put her head down.

"I don't think we should be doing this Terrence."

"I don't think, Chen. I know how I feel," Terrence responded with a raise of his eyebrow pushing his bodice up against the back of Chen as he inhaled the smell of her hair until he nearly lost consciousness.

Terrence took hold of Chen's arm and spun her around to look into his face. He took Chen's hands into his own and put them against his chest.

"You feel that...," Terrence's voice was low and raspy.

Chen bit her lip as she felt a swarm of butterflies tickle her stomach. She couldn't speak. She simply closed her eyes.

"Chen...," Terrence beckoned her for a response. He needed her to understand just how serious he was about his feelings for her. He could hardly stand Gun, and the way he ordered her around. He had long entertained thoughts of ridding the both of them of his presence; but he knew how loyal Chen was to him. Hurting her was the last thing he wanted to do.

Moreover, it was his job to serve and protect Gun. It was his job, nothing more nothing less. He took pride in his loyalty to Gun. It was just about the only trait that could identify his humanity.

Chen brought her hands up to Terrence's face and opened her chocolate eyes to meet his.

"I love you... Terrence?" Chen's forehead wrinkled unsure if her words were forming from pure unfed passions or honest suppressed feelings.

"I do...," Chen continued as if fulfilling a need to convince herself of her profession. "But I must return to Gun. I will die before I would put you in harm's way. I have a duty to my family...my father. I know his death was not in vain."

Terrence stood with a look of deep confusion and frustration. He had no idea what her father had to do with their relationship but he was certain it wasn't a subject he wished to discuss. Terrence felt a lump lock into his throat and then shortly after anger. He was irritated at how reserved Chen could be. She would release such emotion and then withdraw herself from the situation as though she hadn't said something that would change the order of things. There was no way he was going to simply turn and walk away from her after she had expressed her love for him.

Terrence was just as leery of Chen as his nose was open. His senses were heightened around her and Gun. He knew full well Chen was bait for those, Gun had sights on killing. Though there was something different in her eyes. He could see pain and he wanted to soothe the ache that troubled her heart.

Terrence pressed his body up against Chen once more and caused her to fall back into the dark of the pantry. Terrence kept pressing forward urging her to accept him.

"Don't run… Terrence taunted. Chen's hands were shaky and her breath was cut short.

"I'm not running...I just won't surrender my body to you. I can't...," Chen pushed past Terrence grabbing hold to his lean waist. Her legs were weakened as she quickened her pace. She flew from the scene as fast as her legs could carry her. She dare not look back for fear she would run back into the fold of his arms. Her insides burned for him and she knew full well he would quench her every desire but her loyalty to Gun wouldn't let her.

Gun was out running around, tending to business matters more often than not, which left Chen to tend to the duties of the home. Gun didn't trust maids or servants he barely wanted a guard at the door so she was left to cook and clean for herself. Chen made a point to dust each and every corner of their home for fear Gun would find an unclean spot. He would get so angry at the slightest slip of judgment. Accidental spills were unacceptable.

Chen's hands had developed a slight tremor when he was present. She had to grind her teeth to concentrate on steadying herself as not to make Gun nervous. He was beyond paranoid. Cameras were placed in each bedroom of the home to surveillance the inside perimeters of the home. Terrence didn't seem to care about showcasing his advances. Partly, because he was Gun's right hand man and he ran the security around the home. Terrence would lock up and would stand guard until Gun made it home.

Most nights it was just Chen and Terrence. She would cook dinner and they would laugh and joke around while they watched television. Retreating from Terrence's presence was easy at first. She considered him more of a brother to Gun despite his chocolate skin tone. He was beautiful she had to admit that, and he was very respectful and seemed to genuinely care for her feelings.

Chen changed out of her dusty clothes and washed up once more before slipping on her bed clothes. Chen's bedroom door was ajar as usual. From time to time she would see Terrence take a quick peak inside to see that she was ok before he went off to his room. Terrence had a home of his own; but because he was also Chen's body guard he found himself spending most of his nights at Gun's estate.

Terrence had never had a jealous bone in his body. He never held a grudge for too long or had desires to per quire others possessions. He preferred to earn his own keep. His feelings for Chen bothered him more so than he wished to let on because he knew that although he kept her safe, and tended to her daily needs, he knew that she didn't belong to him. Her profession of love sent chills down his spine. Now that he knew of her feelings he felt that it was his duty to protect her from Gun's wrath. He was a ticking time bomb sure to explode any day now due to his half-baked schemes and dirty dealings with the mobs money.

Terrence heard the water going in Chen's bedroom. His mind was busy chanting and encouraging him to check the grounds of the home while his heart and penis are urging him to jump into the shower with Chen. Ultimately he made the decision to check the cameras and lock up. He hadn't expected Gun's return. So he knew that he would be there for the night.

■■■

Chen lay in her king sized bed thinking about Terrence and her near encounter with him just hours before. She tried to put the feel of his muscles under her skin out of her mind, but as much as she tried to forget the thoughts enticed her hormones to play. Chen looked up into the mirror above her bed and closed her eyes as she trailed her fingers along the cleavage of her negligée'. She smiled at her thoughts of Terrence sneaking into her bedroom. She knew that there would be no way she could flee from submitting to her desires.

Chen opened her eyes, as she viewed her body lying on her bed among the crumbled gold satin sheets. The black lace and satin of her night gown felt smooth and tickled her thighs as she playfully teased herself. Chen arched her back as she massaged her inner thigh coaxing her love to moisten the sheets beneath her. She moaned at her seductive play and finally as if she couldn't resist the touch she slid her hands along the lips of her vagina and fondled her pearl in a circular motion. Her actions sent waves of excitement and she began to quiver. Chen called out to Terrence unexpectedly.

Feeling the burn of her desires Chen lost herself in her emotions and became infatuated with her look of ecstasy as she enjoyed the view. Coming out of her coma she flew to the epitome of her sexual climax. Chen moaned and bit her lip in an effort to stifle herself. She heaved and grabbed hold of the sheets as she came too. Chen smiled as she lay back onto her bed and relaxed as her body was still tingling from her playful orchestra.

"Wow...," Terrence finally interjected as he stood at the door of her bedroom. His busty frame leaned up against the cherry wood of the door and his hands were closed as if praying.

Chen's eyes flew open embarrassed about her display and then angered by Terrence's intrusion. Her cheeks were reddened and she couldn't speak. In fact, most of her was still coming down from her personal pleasures.

"You know I could have handled that for you. Watching you is good as tasting you."

Chen grew angry to save face. She was quite embarrassed and the only way to cure the odd feelings was to get mad and throw him out on his ass. Only she wasn't sure he would buy her little breakdown. After all she had called the man's name for Christ's sake. Terrence was far from Gun and if he had been standing there for the entire scene he heard her say his name several times. Chen sat up in her bed and grabbed for her robe.

"Don't...,"Terrence stood up straight and took two paces towards Chen and her bed.

"Terrence..., I want you to leave."

"No you don't...,"

"No..., but I need you to…" Chen was certain she didn't want Terrence to leave but she knew that it was the right thing to do.

"Sh...," Terrence walked up to Chen as she stood to meet his arrival. "Why don't you let me rock you to sleep?"

Chen's eyes twinkled and she looked down towards the floor as she tried to find the answer to his question. She wanted desperately to take him into her arms and have her way with him.

Chen finally looked up into the face of her forbidden lover to respectfully decline his advances.

"Gun will kill you Terrence you had better get your head back in the game."

Terrence lowered his eyes confused about where Chen was going with the conversation because he had clearly heard her say that she loved him. "Believe me my head is in the right place. I need you, and you need me. I promise you this..." Terrence turned on his heels and walked briskly out of Chen's room slamming the door behind him. His emotions were clearly on his sleeve and Chen felt the heat from his eyes burn literal holes into the satin of her gown. She felt low, and full of trickery. She had a need to be loved, hunted, and perhaps even obsessed over. She couldn't lie. She had wanted to feel Terrence inside her for months, but she needed him for far more then sex. Now that she knew he was head over hills. She was sure he would oblige any of her desires.

Just outside Chen's door Terrence threw punches at the wind cursing his initial play date with Chen. He knew he had fucked up big time. He had first tried to sleep with his boss's wife, and then revealed his possible feelings for her husband's demise. He may have screwed himself two ways from Sunday. Though it seemed they both had secrets to hide from dear old Gun. Chen was the mastermind of seduction. He was just a pawn in her tangled weave of deception and desire.

Terrence's thirst for Chen was unquenchable he wasn't sure he could take no for an answer the slanderous nature of their relationship intensified his erotic thoughts to play. His mind was murderous.

Dirty Deeds....Chen pulled her chicken from

the oven. She was preoccupied in her attempt to rid the aroma of adultery from her family home. Chen took comfort in the fact that she wasn't able to have children. She wouldn't dare bring anything else into Gun's fascist way of living. He was a poor leader, more of a bully in Chen's eyes.

Chen set the table and retreated to her bedroom to get ready for Gun's arrival. She was just getting ready to light the candles when she felt Gun's sweaty chest greasing up the back of her silk robe. She could smell his stench. Chen forced a smile and spun herself around.

"Not so fast lover boy, can we eat first?"

"I want you," Gun leaned in and licked the tip of Chen's nose. It nearly made her stumble back on to the table. She was disgusted that he had put his tongue onto her person.

"Do you now? " Gun was excited to see Chen after his fun filled day at the warehouse. He had gone on a rather exciting killing spree and he could think of nothing better than to end his night with a hot fresh piece of untainted ass. Sloppy seconds was never his cup of tea. He enjoyed the pleasures of a raunchy show once in a while during the night hours on Hollywood boulevard.

That evening Gun had a surprise for her. He collected on his winnings from various gambling stations and paid visits to those that seemed to forget that they owed him. Gun sprinkled cash all over the front of Chen's bosom as he galloped around her singing Little Wayne's, "Duffle Bag Boy." Gun's accent was still left back in Korea and had yet to pick up any swag as he kept his country boy two step. Chen found his rendition quite funny, but her thoughts were well away.

Chen had Terrence on the brain. She was fixated on his chocolate skin, his perfect smile, and the ass wasn't a bad look either. Chen felt belittled by the fact that she even had to continue sleeping with Gun in order to keep the peace in her home; but this was one of her wifely duties. She was the daughter of a well-known gangster, a mob figure, but also one that was more than some thug of the streets. He was generous in nature, and preferred to be called, "God Father," a concept he'd grown to adopt from one of his favorite Italian films.

Chen thought about Terrence and the way he liked to crack jokes about her ghetto booty, as she danced around the floor of her Living room enticing Gun's nature to rise. Terrence always said Chen wasn't working with the traditional Asian ass she was packing a little junk in her trunk, an ass that jiggled when she walked and clapped on cue when she danced seductively. He wanted to taste her so bad he often imagined the feel of her soft clit massaging his tongue.

Terrence was fixated at how a pure Asian girl could rock so smoothly, he was sure there was some black in her family. They were burning in heat for one another. Chen was fearful that she would call out to Terrence during her session with Gun.

Chen closed her eyes and swallowed hard as she coaxed Gun towards the cream and gold colored love seat in their living room by his tie. Gun was licking his tongue and salivating as he dragged sluggishly behind like a dog in heat. Chen snarled at Gun to stir his juices. Gun barked at attention. It was an awful choice Chen decided as his face turned into something demonic. She was sure then that she was sleeping with one the devil's own angels.

Chen whipped Gun around to face her and threw Gun down unto the soft cushions. Gun licked his lips and scooted down into the seat to a comfortable position. Taunting Chen to take notice to his hard penis he gyrated, his pelvis to showcase his manhood standing at attention.

Chen smiled a crooked seductive smile as she put the spike of her heel to Gun's chest. Sliding her heel down the silk of his shirt she slowly popped the buttons exposing the ripple of his chest. Chen's red lipstick sparkled in the glow of the dim lighting. She was feeling herself and well in tune with the music. In heat and needing to cool her desires, Chen let go of her inhibitions and straddled the top of Gun's face. His head fell back into the head of the seat as he awaited her descent.

Chen's breath was hot and sweet. She was dipping and swirling her hips instigating an attack. Gun inhaled deeply and scooted up towards the opening of Chen's thighs. Hoping to get a whiff of Chen's, punani he was itching to whip is tongue around the pearl of her love to suckle its juices.

Chen nearly threw up in her mouth at the sight of Gun's atrocious vulgarity. He was a sickening display. She looked away briefly to slip back into character. Snapping back robotically she forged her way in. Chen walked six paces from Gun and urged him to join her with a cunning gesture, her middle finger. Gun was turned on by Chen's loutish display. He bit his lip and jumped up like a puppet on a string. He was rock solid and could hardly take anymore of Chen's torment.

Chen's thoughts were so far away from Gun. She was uncontrollably fixated, on Terrence. His hands had touched every inch of her body in less than a minute. Chen could see flashes of the two of them so vividly as if she were watching a movie. Her insides still burned with lust at the thought of their foreplay. Her fingers tingled, with warm sensations. She tried to put away her thoughts of Terrence but his bulging chest was a constant reminder of the sensation she received in just those moments of pure bliss.

She had fallen prey to her selfish desires, and had feelings of guilt behind her adulterous actions. Still, Chen had hopes of saving her marriage with Gun. She had respect for her father and his wishes and though he was gone, she had every belief that he still knew of her actions. Chen knowingly accepted Terrence's advances and she enjoyed her time spent with him. The betrayal came easy however, when she found evidence of foul play in relation to her father. She could barely shake the notion from her brow when in his presence. He reeked of malice.

Chen felt her hands wrapping around the flesh of his neck. She was gripping Gun's trachea applying pressure as Gun begged her for more. Chen's eyes darkened and for a moment she lost her wits. She could taste blood. Chen licked her lips like a blood thirsty hound. She was turned on by Gun's loss of consciousness. As if Gun had panicked he, grabbed hold of her wrist. It startled her a bit but she was able to jump back into character without notice.

Chen imagined popping the buckle of Terrence's slacks, as she physically removed Gun's. Her nipples hardened. Chen's mind was at play. Her heart skipped a beat, and she could swear she would die if she didn't get a taste of his love. Chen pictured her mouth engulfing the head and shaft of Terrence's penis. She smiled as she twined and heaved her hips in a small interlude while she undressed him.

Gun was so eager to get it in. He stood up abruptly as Chen pulled his belt from his pants. Chen closed her eyes trying to maintain her view of Terrance just as Gun grabbed hold to her face and rammed his slimy tongue down her throat.

"I am going to fuck the shit out of you." Gun groaned as he held on to Chen maintaining his firm grip. Chen slightly pounced backwards. His tongue was too wet as if filled with fungus. She was sick to her stomach. The ecstasy pill was wearing off or simply not strong enough to subdue her ill thoughts of intimacy with Gun, a man she had loved for so long.

She could hardly stomach him now. The necklace brought about memory's she would rather forget. The fact that the necklace was in his possession poisoned her view of him instantly. No matter the explanation. Chin wondered if she could trust Terrence as well. She poured out some of her deepest and darkest secrets hoping to win his trust and respect. His expressions of love could have just as easily been fabricated to prove his loyalty to Gun. Chen couldn't be sure if Gun set the stage for her and Terrence to become intimate only to prove her disloyalty. She was filled with anxiety. Every time Gun went to answer his phone or the door, Chen became nervous that Terrence would expose her. Caught red handed before her plan could unfold.

Chen couldn't be sure why she didn't trust Terrence with her life. He could have turned the tables on her some time ago. It wasn't their first time in such close proximity but it was the most intimate. His breath danced around the tendrils of her hair blowing them just enough to tickle her cheeks as he whispered sweet nothings into her ear. Her fingers tickled the breast of his chest. This time was different, not like the times before, the take-out dinners and movies as they waited for Guns homecoming. He was Chen's babysitter nothing more.

They did things brothers and sisters did, tease one another and compete for the last slice of pizza. Chen and Terrence laughed the night away as they imitated Gun's persona during meetings with men. Him and his God father walk and, *"Scarface,"* accent during his long winded speeches. Chen played back the idea of Terrence being no more than a friend, just a member of the family, but her memory of Terrence was far too potent to meet the line of innocence. Their passions had long since crossed those borders. Chen's thoughts surged through her veins as the heat bellowed out from her slightly parted lips, down the front of her sheer blouse and cupped the mouth of her panties. Sparks flew as their mouths touched. Terrence was making love to her and had yet to feel the soft, wet tissues that warmed the inner depths of her thighs.

Meanwhile in Chen's present time Gun was thrusting and power driving her small frame through her satin panties. She was so wet from her reminisce of her and Terrence's rendezvous, Gun felt the showering of Chen's love as his own doing. He was excited. Chen chimed back into what seemed to be a low budget porno on steroids, trying desperately to hang onto her arousal; but guns breath smelled of salami and booze.

Gun didn't seem to mind her quiet over exaggerated moans he was nearing climax and preferred to get his nut and drool on through the night. Chen counted him down in her mind as well, looking forward to a hot shower and tall glass of wine.

Power of Persuasion...Terrence paced the floor of his

guest bedroom listening to Chen's charade with Gun. His insides burned. He wanted to kill Gun right then and there and strangle the shit out of Chen for submitting to him. He knew he couldn't rat her out he was in too deep. He had fallen head over heels, and was in no way prepared to deal with what came with sharing a woman.

Terrence had secrets as well. Secrets that could ruin the relationship he was hoping to build on with Chen. His past was worse than Gun's. He had a choice, bright young football star in college with a great head on his shoulders until his little brother was gunned down on his way home from school. He never woke up from that nightmare. He spent his entire adult life angry at the world and felt as though making others suffer would put an end to the hurt and betrayal he felt in his own heart. At least until he started to move past the dark clouds that hovered over him to see what Chen was really up to, investigating her intentions gave room for redemption. She was looking for justice and this was something new to him. No one cared that his brother Damien was killed in broad daylight just two blocks from his school. It was just another black boy murdered at the hands of another, "Gang Violence," school officials and news headlines said; but Terrence knew the truth.

Chen opened his eyes to the world and the political facets of it all. She told him all about her culture and the gruesome rituals about life as a Korean woman. Terrence knew her family and had an opinion of his own about how the women were treated; but he never urged his feelings to care. He couldn't afford to linger into other concerns that had no direct link to his own unless it involved money. For as long as he was affiliated with the Chang family his presence was just a job, nothing more. Terrence would listen to Chen's stories and dream that he was there. He felt her pain and wanted to share his life from the very beginning but he couldn't be sure that Chen could be trusted either.

Terrence mulled over the idea that Chen was just using him for bait. She could have said the same thing for him. After all, he was Gun's right hand man. His initial job was to protect him and his money, not his wife. If things got too sticky Chen herself knew that Gun would throw her to the wolves. He had spoken to Terrence a number of times about getting rid of Chen if it weren't for her money.

Terrence looked into the mirror over his cherry wood chest of drawers peering into his reflection. He was contemplating his intentions with Chen himself, her money wasn't a bad look but he wasn't broke. Aside, from his undercover work as a mob figure his day job brought about great pleasure.

Terrence was the head chef for the Biltmore Hotel, nestled in the busy streets of Downtown Los Angeles. Coming to America helped pave a path that Terrence could be proud of. He wanted so badly to lose the gun holster and three-piece get up it was killing him. He had dressed down to a leather bomber and street jeans, and urban look he felt could help him adjust and blend in more.

He waited for the jokes to flow across tables about his past life. He was born and raised in Korea. Most of the African American citizens could hardly believe it until he spoke the language. Terrence had learned to use a sword and the art of martial arts long before he picked up a hand gun. He was the lucky one. His mother was ill most of her life and his father was never around It was just him and his aunt in Korea, the rest of his family lived in South Central Los Angeles, a place he vowed never to return to after his brother's murder.

Times change, and with the changes in season, circumstances landed him back into the land he pledged to leave in his past. Terrence's stomach dropped as he called his attention to Gun's senseless moaning and Chen's taunting. He clenched his fists, cocking them back and punching at the air stopping just inches from shattering the glass mirror. Terrence felt pains in his chest that may have justified symptoms of a heart attack. He wasn't interested in having it checked out. He was dying from a broken heart. Terrence began to sweat his naked chest heaving in an effort to catch his breath.

"Karma is a bitch," Terrence gurgled as he coughed and panted grabbing hold to the corner of his dresser. His eyes were black as night, his pupils fully dilated. Terrence began to panic but he didn't want to call out for help for fear he may not truly get any. Terrence grabbed for his glass of water just seconds before collapsing onto the bedroom floor. The glass pounced onto the carpet and the water spilled soaking up any evidence of foul play.

■ ■

Chen confirmed the quiet in both her bedroom and Terrence's room before she made an attempt to get down to business. She didn't have the time to be bothered with Terrence's questions so she was sure to put a little something extra in his water as well. It wasn't two minutes after Gun's head hit the pillow before he was sound asleep. He slept like a bear in hibernation. Chen stood over Gun's head taunting him to assure he was in a deep sleep before she left the room. He rarely needed the help of drugs to fall asleep; but just to be sure she wasn't interrupted she gave him a little dose of Trazadone as well.

Chen peaked into Terrence's room. She was alarmed at his position and decided it best to check his pulse. He wasn't a fan of meds and if he ever had to visit a doctor's office he would be kicking and screaming. Chen giggled slightly at the sight of Terrence's overgrown ass struggling with doctors about a measly vaccination.

After making sure the new love of her life was still alive and well, Chen retreated from the room slowly and closed the door as soft as she could careful not to stir him. Chen had to work fast if she was going to make the plan work. Her murderous letters worked like a charm. Now it was time to really put some fear in Gun's heart. She was going to retrieve the necklace from amongst his treasures and place them by his gun holster and jacket in his office. She was also going to have a look see at the two letters marked, "P.1 and P.2."

Chen quickly moved into Gun's office and got to work. She placed the necklace strategically by his belongings and then went to open the two letters. She couldn't believe her eyes as she read the headline and the beneficiary.

"Insurance policies…" Chen's forehead wrinkled and her eyes were as wide as she could brighten them. Gun had taken a life insurance policy out on her father for over two million dollars. Chen read as she thought about why she hadn't had any knowledge of the insurance policy.

"The beneficiary of said insurance policy will be awarded to Gun Sun, son n law to Mr. Chang, as his daughter is unable to accept such responsibilities due to her declining health. " Chen's mouth flew open as she continued to read the letter of lies. Flipping from page to page of the scandalous plot she soon found the cashed check stub folded neatly and stapled to the back of the policy.

"He cashed in on my father's death…," Chen whispered to herself. Her hands shaking so nervously she couldn't be sure she wouldn't slice him that very evening as he slept. She could only speculate that the other envelope contained a policy with her name on it. She too, was living on borrowed time. Chen knew that when his well ran dry, he would be in search for funds to cover his lifestyle.

Chen leaned back in Gun's over-sized leather chair and closed her eyes. She didn't know what she was going to do but she had to think fast. Gun was going crazy but not quick enough. She had already started pulling her assets from Gun's firm hold; but she was under his radar. Terrence had been a Godsend. He threw Gun from sniffing out her dirt plenty of times, still she didn't know whether Terrence would wait until the head dick in charge was out of commission before he collected his debt from her or just killed her and ran with the money.

Terrence seemed like he had, had a rough childhood himself, but coming to the states was a good thing for him. The change of climate calmed his nerves a bit. Just how much Chen couldn't be sure, Chen was taking a big chance on Terrence. Her feelings for him had grown from lust to love in just weeks. Though she could tell that something was bothering Terrence. He wouldn't talk about it. He always assured her that he was fine. She hoped that they both weren't playing the waiting game. It would all end horribly, a blood bath she would be sure to fire first in. She wasn't going to take the chance of Terrence or Gun killing her before she could see the look in Gun's eyes when she revealed that she knew of his murderous betrayal.

Gun's change of scenery however only made matters worse for him and the paranoia a good fit to float her plan. The Korean's of her homeland hadn't found them yet but she did a good job pretending they had. Chen sent letters out to Korea. She used her cousin to send them right back unopened. They were ruthless, graphical, and murderous threats she wrote threatening both herself and Gun. She wanted the terrorizations to appear as authentic as possible.

Chen had told her cousin that she was sending correspondence to some business associates in America with regards to the opening of her restaurant; but she didn't want Gun to find out about her plans because he was

A i j a   M .

abusive. The truth was that she just wanted the letters sent to their home from Korea.

The plan worked. Gun was so spooked he rarely left the home unless his presence was absolutely needed. When he did leave the home he left packed with guns in every place of concealment he could manage to carry, a personal driver, and two body guards.

He took on spending his nights in his office. He watched the surveillance cameras until his eyes dried. The internet was his best friend. Gun spent countless hours researching his men looking for any evidence of betrayal. Gun was the actual heathen of the bunch. He had some nerve researching the backgrounds of others. To Chen he was the prime suspect, the only suspect even.

Chen had taken to the city of angels quite nicely. In her ventures out into the world of glam and fame, she had managed to grab hold of a piece of real estate she could call her own. Terrence was often in tow, as he was her body guard and Gun's spy. As their relationship blossomed her material wealth became plural; something she didn't mind. She longed for a real family and took comfort in the fact that Terrence wasn't worried about their difference in race and culture. He was more than willing to start a family with her. The guilt however, was filling both their hearts. He felt like he was betraying Gun in the worst way. He wasn't stealing money. He was sneaking around with his most prize possession, the love of his life.

Chen wasn't innocent either. She felt the urge to confess many a day but she fought her consciousness between the lines of love and loyalty. Ultimately she found herself locked in the confines of both elements, being that her fight was between the love of her life and her father. The love for her father filled her heart and she felt the nudge to holster a gun. She knew that she would die trying to avenge her father's murder, no matter the face uncovered for this ultimate sin. She had the intention of burning Terrence in his own lustful fires as well but her feelings melted by the flames he himself preserved. If she was taken by the qualms of love and her deceitful heart she would get her just desserts. She couldn't even be mad about such a price to pay. As long as she died with honor, her only wish as of late.

Chen quickly put away her stolen treasures making sure the policies appeared untouched. She slipped quietly into the confines of her master bedroom and slid into bed next to the enemy. Her stomach rumbled in detest as she lay by her adversary. Unsure she would be able to play her charade much longer she lay contemplating her next move. One that she hoped would come to her soon before Gun figured her out and struck first.

Drag me to hell... Terrence woke up

from his drug induced coma to find his limbs so sore he could barely move. He searched his surroundings and found nothing out of the ordinary to consider an attempt at foul play. He was however oblivious as to why his limbs ached and he was lying on the floor.

Terrence tried to free himself from his vulnerable state. He was unsuccessful the first time around but was triumphant in his second attempt. Pulling himself onto his knees he gasped for air and couldn't believe that such a person of good health could perspire so easily. After regaining his composure, he threw on a muscle tee, and went in search of the home. He couldn't be sure if someone had managed to sneak in for a surprise kill or a simple robbery. Terrence grabbed both his semi-automatic and his long nose nine millimeters and took cover as he eased open his bedroom door. His feet were planted firmly onto the floor as he tip toed about the cabin.

Chen was fast asleep lying next to Gun. Terrence sniffed and left the room quietly before his anger took him over. He could kill in that moment. He was in desperate need of a new venture. Chen's shenanigans were sure to get them both killed. Her mind set was sketchy.

Terrence ignored his feelings and continued canvasing the home. He searched Gun's office for misplaced items and the downstairs area. Finally confident that whatever had gone down with him passing out was an inside job he retreated back to his room. The cameras were clear of any suspicious characters looking to flee or descend upon them. Now his mind plagued him with ideas of Chen betraying him. Why would she drug him? Didn't she believe in his love for her? He too, questioned her intentions but she had nothing to gain but a loving and trusting relationship, rather than Gun's violent sadistic behaviors.

Terrence lay in his bed looking at the ceiling. His arms and legs were still sore but he welcomed the pain. It was an inclination that he was still human. In his line of work he often forgot. Chen was the reason for his transformation as of late; but if his love story ending was nothing but a hoax he couldn't be sure of how his reaction to the news would be. They all could be in danger including him. His stability was based on the trust that he developed with Chen. His past was no longer a factor of his present. He was learning to build new and healthy relationships despite how he acquired his love.

Terrence could shit straight blood. His mind drifted in and out of anger and love for Chen. It truly was a thin line between love and hate. As he laid there pondering what had occurred in the hours of his slumber his heart ached at possible betrayal, and his love rose behind the excitement of their betrayal in regards to Gun. His anger preceded compassion and his recent folly with love hadn't changed his composure. Terrence was sure it was Chen that drugged him but he needed to know why. So she didn't trust him, so why all the sneaking around, as if they were going to be together? Terrence was beginning to think that he was the bait in Chen's plan.

Had Chen used him from the start after all she was good at persuading men to do just what she wanted them to? His mind wandered back into his days of vengeance and it poured right into anger.

"I swear to God if she played me I will cut her ass up and fucking feed her to the dogs." Terrence was grinding his teeth so hard his jaw bone was visible. His mind was a terrible thing. His conscious flew back and forth into the dangers of his past and screamed for redemption.

Terrence clenched his fists tightly without taking notice to his pocket knife slicing into his flesh. Blood was peeking through his overgrown palms; but Terrence continued. His eyes fell closed as his reminiscent views of Chen played back in his mind. He rubbed his head against his shoulder and shuddered for a moment as if tickled by her hair. Terrence felt a warm sensation flow through him as love filtered his heart once again. He realized he was gone weakened and marked for dead. He had blown his own cover. The only thing he could hope was that she was sincere in her feelings for him.

■ ■

Chen lye in her bed next to Gun wishing she was in the room down the hall. She heard Terrence peak in and the smack of his lips as he left. He was irritated she could tell and searching for answers. She had grown to know Terrence well. He was an open book when it came to the matters of security. It was his personal attributes that were buried treasures. Chen felt the heat rise up her nighty and arouse her juices to flow. She clenched her legs tight to avoid the advance of sexual provocation but she was unsuccessful.

Chen wanted so very badly to leap from her king sized bed and run to the open arms of Terrence. Still she wasn't certain he would welcome her. The guilt out poured as she recollected the events of the night. Her stomach rumbled and this time she was unable to holster the vomit fuming into her throat. Barely making it to her master bathroom she threw up the contents of her stomach until all that remained was bile.

Chen wanted nothing more than to be solely with Terrence but not before she avenged her father. She was close to answers and couldn't afford to flee from the truth now. Chen wondered if Terrence was strong enough to endure the true situation but to fire him would raise too many eyebrows.

Gun was a stupid little man. He seemed to think that no one would or could ever cross him. He was at the center of attention and had the crown. Of course people wanted his head on a silver platter. He was a criminal too. Her father wasn't. He was a business man and always fought for the fairness of his people. Gun stole from his people, those that trusted and followed him. His greed gave him plenty motive to have killed her father. She just wanted him to say the words. Chen had every intention of murdering Gun. Once she knew for sure he was behind the dirty deed. She willed to run right to his men and ask about the venture; but she couldn't show her face in Korea thanks to his thieving ass.

Trust was a big issue with the Korean mob family, a rule of thumb Chen's father always reiterated. Gun mistook power. He forgot the element of respect which called his men to ponder over throwing his leadership. Chen shook her head as she collapsed into a ball of exhaustion. She was glad that while in her cleaning frenzy, she'd managed to spruce around the toilet seat and base. Gun was poor at aiming for the inside of the toilet, no wonder he needed a flock of men to do his dirty work for him.

Chen lay by her toilet in the bathroom sure she had thrown up a lung, her guilt also. She felt no need to feel sorry for someone that took her father's life. He wasn't the best man he made mistakes but he was her father and he was loyal to his cause and people. The Chang's for the most part were one of the most respected families in North Korea, respect that was genuine and not derived from fear.

Chen's father taught her that, *a man that fears will never be respected; but one that fears not will gain the respect of his men by his fearless actions.* Chen held his words close especially when the wrath of Gun was upon her. She used the fear she had for Gun and stifled herself when he demanded her to submit to him and showcase his power over her. She felt so much pain during his explosive beatings. Still, Chen held her ground and endured the horrific pounding. It took every bone in Terrence's body not to break Guns face when he put his hands on Chen well before their love affair even began.

It would all come to an end soon. Those thoughts of peace and redemption fell over Chen and made her feel comforted by her father's lingering presence. Chen often thought about her brother as well. He wasn't much in the brawn area but was intelligent. Something most men missed out on in their voyage to success.

Chen's brother, Chang-sun could talk a man out of his life savings without the raise of a hand. Which was another reason his choice of lifestyle hurt their father. He was gay and though unspoken by most he was open about his sexual preference. Chang-son had intimate talks about his desires with her all the time. Chen thought that his life style was so liberating it was new and exciting. She couldn't wait to hear the stories of her brother's new love or sexual encounter. She didn't see the harm in finding love because back then she and Gun were so in love they truly were the picture perfect couple. She could share her joy with not only her brother but her best friend aside from Gun.

Chen had never been close to her mother. Her mother was far more interested in her father's money. She was conniving. That ability she inherited directly from her mother but she was able to channel it. At least she thought. Chen was beat and tortured into a frenzy of confused emotions. She was trained to suppress her thoughts and feelings, her intentions weren't her own. Chen had to follow and respect the rules of her husband or suffer the consequences. She ventured into different lands and her father's social status allowed her to attend schools of higher education. It wasn't the country rule the dictator fascist ways of life were her husbands. It was true that her dad wished his son could be his successor; he denounced that fact as soon as he saw his son's true colors. From then on Chang-sun was stripped of his name. He was an outcast, left to the streets.

Unlike most Korean women Chen was very advanced in knowledge of the western culture. She learned most from her brother. He dreamed of moving to San Francisco. There wasn't much she could learn from a book. She procured tourists from the states and enjoyed meeting student's that were from different countries. Most were students of international business. Chen thought they were boring. Their usual conversation consisted of demographics and companies in good or bad standing. She did learn that most men were fixated on money no matter the culture or mode of origin. Just as long as they had power because after all money equates power.

Chen laughed as she mimicked how her brother used to prance around her bedroom making fun of his economics teacher, much like the way her and Terrence cracked jokes on Gun. He was as smart as a stupid person could be. He knew just about too much for his own good a default on any chance for growth. Chen's father always told her that it was important to be teachable.

"It isn't necessarily true that you live and die by the sword. It was quite possible to live smart and die with old age. The difference in the sword is its stroke. The areas you expose your weapon. Like a game of cards. You don't just openly show your hand you may want to bluff a bit, with the full intent on following through with your threat."

Gun was openly frugal about his ability to summon his men to kill or claim what he felt was owed to him. He lacked tenacity and finesse in his business. Something he used to listen to Chen about but; as of late he was just the head *dick* in charge, nothing more in all aspects of the word.

Chen looked saddened as she thought about how her and Gun used to be. At one point and time Gun was fighting for freedom as well and preached to her father about allowing her to attend college. Chen didn't want to be the usual Korean gal working in nail shops or boutiques selling bootleg designer purses and shoes. She wanted the all American dream. She wasn't a feminist either. She enjoyed male companionship and she didn't mind him making the decisions from time to time. Her and Gun were in agreement on most things back then, she was actually a part of the decision making process. Things had changed dramatically once Gun started working for her father. He was mean, angry, and had a secret lust and thirst for money. Soon after, his employment Chen knew she had lost Gun love to greed and money.

It took her years to actually admit this fact to herself. Even the beatings she excused to his fragile minds torment. She felt like the job was too overwhelming and he just needed help. The death of her father is what brought about questions of dishonor. Things didn't add up. Where were his guards? Why hadn't anyone received a distress call?

Chen knew from the very start it had to have been an inside job. He knew his killer well. Chen's eyes began to well with tears as she played the events of her father's funeral in the window of her bedroom. She saw the rain pouring and the solemn faces of his business partners in plain view. She was all that was left. Except the fact that Gun was now her husband and he stood next in line to inherit the business through his connection with her. Nothing as treacherous ever crossed her mind in the years before until Guns change in persona took form. Chen had searched the faces of each and every man there except Guns and his right hand man that stood on either side of her.

Terrence was Gun's right hand, the man she now loved and cherished with all her heart, a change that she could never imagine but one that she welcomed freely. Chen kicked herself emotionally for not looking deep into her mind to see all the signs pointing to Gun before. As the saying says, *"Love is blind."* Now, however her eyes were open.

The rain seemed to wash away the picture of her father she envisioned as she looked off into her large window. The curtains were open and the rain patted gently against the glass. As though her memory was being wiped clean. Chen's fathers face vanished like a smeared painting as the drops ran down the glass of her window.

Chen sat up in bed unable to stomach her ties with Gun. He had betrayed her in the worst way. The man she once trusted with her life had not only taken the life of her father but he had plans to kill her as well. It was just a matter of time.

The night seemed longer than ever. Chen couldn't sleep if she wanted to. After she planted evidence and plotted against her husband one last time she had built up quite a hunger. Chen thought about how nice a Turkey and Swiss sandwich would be; but she didn't want to alarm Gun in case he woke up looking for her. She was surprised she wasn't presently smothered. He nearly suffocated her with his arms and legs wrapped around her torso so tight it was a wonder she could breathe. Gun shackled her so that he could detect any movement during the night. Even her trips to the bathroom were calculated and under surveillance.

Gun had developed a lack of trust in her as well. He needed to know her every thought. Those that didn't follow his ruling were eliminated. Gun believed Chen was envious of his relationship with her father. He said that she too would try and take him down due to her greed and temptress mannerisms.

He was sure she plotted against him after his inheritance of her father's business. Though Gun hadn't really inherited anything, he stole it. Chen vowed that with her dying breath she would prove it. She often battled her emotions about doing away with her childhood friend and lover but he wasn't the man she had fallen in love with. He was a murdering thief. The grumbles of Chen's stomach interrupted her thoughts. So she decided that she needed to make that run down stairs for an early morning snack.

Suddenly, her hunger overpowered her fear of Gun. She was going to go down to the kitchen before her insides ate themselves, whether he woke up or not. Chen got up confidently and made her way to her bathroom to fetch her robe and slippers. She was hoping to run into Terrence. Just for maybe a few words of love and playful flirting. The dangers of their love affair were so intoxicating she played with the idea of Gun catching the two of them in action. What would he do then? She toyed with her wants of putting the pieces back together again. The love she had for gun was pixelated but she had not forgotten how good it felt to be loved and respected by a man of like cultures.

Terrence was something fresh and new. He was raised in Korea; but he was every bit African American and proud of it. No matter his confirmation of Korean culture he was a black man with the same black man ethic. The white man was out to get him. It was true for Terrence. His line of work ensured that men of all races wanted him dead. He was a ruthless assassin. Men and women were at his disposal. They weren't his problem. Money was money and the heart beats he stopped were procedure nothing personal. Terrence's personal life was just that a secret he kept locked away in Pandora's Box.

Chen plopped down stairs and flip flopped about the kitchen. She threw open her invisible fridge door and grabbed just about every sandwich meat, cheese, and condiment, there was. She threw a slice of peppered Turkey into her mouth and scooped her arms around the goods tightening her grip. She didn't want to make too much noise.

Chen used her leg to kick the refrigerator door closed. She spun around briskly and nearly lost her footing as she heaved the contents of her arms onto the marble topped island of the kitchen. Terrence was standing just in back of her. He watched her every move. She hadn't heard his approaching footsteps. Terrence licked his lips. He enjoyed the view. Chen was dancing about seductively while she made her creation.

"Looks like you worked up quite an appetite."

Chen was startled as she spun around ready to attack her assailant at whim. "Shit Terrence you scared me."

"I bet…" Terrence's face was stern and plain. It changed Chen's persona immediately. She suddenly looked solemn and then frustrated that he couldn't just let the events of the night simmer away in the darkness. She wasn't exactly proud of herself.

"Not now," Chen said through her grinding teeth. She didn't want to relive the events of the night. She just wanted her sandwich and maybe some plain Lay's on the side. All the talk about her frolic with Gun was beginning to ruin her appetite.

"I get it. You're angry with me"

"Damn straight. Sleeping with Gun is more than the issue baby. It's the fact that you drugged me. Any explanation as to why you felt the need to play me?

"Umm let me see partly to avoid this. I didn't play you Terrence. This stand off right here is exactly the reason I made sure to put a little something in your drink. It wasn't to hurt you. I was trying to protect you. Looks like it didn't work, because here you are questioning me about sleeping with my husband." Chen enunciated every syllable. She was clearly over exaggerating her terms and Terrence was near his breaking point between domestic violence and his new found gentle giantess.

Terrence snatched half of Chen's sandwich as she cut it ever so delicately and slammed it down his throat. She was more than bothered by it. Her stomach had caved in since her last meal. She and gun didn't get the chance to eat the dinner she made. By the time she felt the urge to eat, she didn't have the stomach for a full course meal.

Terrence didn't say another word to Chen. He grabbed a few of the chips that danced around her lonely half sub as if the plate belonged to him. Terrence rolled his eyes and left her standing there with a bewildered expression on her face. Chen didn't know what Terrence's intentions were. He was angry and cocky. She knew and loved that characteristic about him. It was a foolish notion to think of Terrence as calm and collected. He appeared so sincere just before his kills.

Chen didn't like the situation any more than he did; but what the fuck could she do? The man was her husband. She had a plan yes, but it was far from over. The truth was Chen hadn't worked up the courage to pull an actual weapon on Gun. She needed him to admit to the truth, she just didn't have the balls to do it just yet she wasn't really prepared to hear the truth.

Chen wanted to run after Terrence. She didn't... for fear she would draw Gun's attentions to stir.

Terrence secretly prayed she would. Just to prove her love for him. He'd take her right in the hall to his bedroom. He could taste the sweet nectar of her breasts and his mouth began to water. Terrance laughed to himself. He would show Gun how to make love to a woman. He joked to himself about having his way with Chen all over his mansion.

Terrence rolled his head sarcastically as he thought about Chen's audacity to bring up her right to consummate with her husband. Terrence went to slam his door and caught it just before it met the sill. He didn't want to ruin a possible encounter if she decided to stop by and say goodnight. He was angry but not that mad.

He knew it was wishful thinking but he couldn't help his desires. His love was rising, and if he had to Terrence had no fear in the event he was forced to face Gun about their love affair. Terrence had all but said that he was

A i j a   M .

in love with Chen. Gun was so selfish and blind. It was time he got a taste of his own medicine. He was so busy stealing from his men, he left his yard unattended. The gate was open and Terrence walked right in. Getting rid of Gun was on top of his list as well. Maybe not for the same reason Chen had in mind. Terrence and Chen may each have a different motive; but the end result was the same. Gun's head on a silver platter, Terrence was tired of sharing Chen. If her plan didn't come to a head soon, he was going to have to take matters into his own hands.

Death Sentence..., *the seven*

deadly sins were descending upon Chen's conscience and Gun was sure to feel the wrath of her vengeance. Gun's smug look of fearlessness had yet to shatter. An explosion couldn't take the heat off him as Chen buried her eyes into Gun's deceitful eyes. He looked so confident standing there, enjoying Chen's hesitation to spew her whereabouts. Chen was fearful, but fearful of her own actions in regards to Gun's well-being. She couldn't be sure she could hold back her desire to slit his throat before the questions she demanded answers to were acknowledged.

Chen was determined to show Gun that her fear of him had gone. She meant business and his playful sarcasm wasn't going to do either of them any good. She was in charge and she would be the one to demand the answers probing her brow. He just didn't know it yet.

Chen wasn't sure she had an answer for Gun. He was standing in front of her leaning his head against the wall. She was surprisingly calm. Gun was doing his best to scare her. He held his pocket knife close to his tongue. He cut his apple seductively and stared at Chen so hard she could feel the burn. She didn't know what to say about the necklace. She just hadn't worked that part out. Gun asked Chen once more where she had gone off to early that morning.

She was so taken back by Gun's new jewelry piece she couldn't find the words. Chen felt like she would pass out if she didn't get to the bathroom soon. He was asking all the wrong questions, and he didn't appear to be at all freaked out that this piece of jewelry he was wearing belonged to her deceased father.

Chen couldn't believe her eyes. She wanted to be sure she was actually living out her worst fears. Gun was standing right in her face wearing her father's necklace like he was entitled to his legacy. He was showing off his winnings from the kill. Something Chen couldn't stomach. Right then and there she had all the evidence she needed to put an end to Gun's reign over her. She was about to set the record straight right then and there.

Gun was standing there with his bald chest waiting for an explanation as to her whereabouts early that morning. Chen's face was hot and turning red. Her rage was burrowing inside. Gun thought for sure it was time to step in and slap the taste out of Chen's mouth. He was anxious to commence his beating as he was sure she was with another man. Just as soon as she tried to spit out a lie he was planning on laying her ass out right in the middle of the kitchen floor. He knew she wasn't home when he got out of bed that morning, and he knew she wasn't with any of her friends. The few she'd managed to hold on to that is. Gun was such a nasty individual many of her friends threatened to end their friendship if she didn't make a decision to leave him.

Gun stood up straight and popped his knuckles. Chen stood her ground this time and lowered her eyes. Gun was instantly enraged at Chen's bold stance. He demanded an answer once more after he let out a bellowing laugh.

"I see you are feeling adventurous today. It must be the change of scenery. Don't let America get you killed Chen. Answer my damn question or you will be sorry. Gun took two steps closer to Chen after he plunged his pocket knife into the basket of fruit sitting on the kitchen island.

Chen had been gone all morning. She went to check on her apartment. She also had an interview with the local hospital in Long Beach, but for the first time since her ventures out into the world she took care of her business solo. She didn't need Terrence to show her around town anymore and she for sure didn't want any of Gun's men escorting her to and fro. Chen took her car. She drove her car, and she was very proud of herself.

Chen didn't give a shit what his thoughts on the matter were but she was sure he would try and ruin any hopes a future. Chen felt her fist clench as Gun motioned towards her once more. She wasn't going down without a fight this time. She had, had enough of Gun. She knew all she needed to know to put an end to Gun once and for all. The only problem now, was Terrence. After their confrontation he was very distant. His actions made her nervous. She just couldn't tell if she could trust him any longer or if he had grown soft and now plotted against her as well. Either way she had one mission and that was to get her confession from Gun.

She was ready to admit to her pranks and tom foolery that ultimately led up to his break in mental stability. He had long since ruined his business. His goon's were trickling like a man with a bladder deficiency. Gun didn't have much clout. The boys were fully aware and because of his present business transactions failing royally, they questioned his every demand.

Terrence was the only loyal one since before their hooking up. His eyes often grew teary when he thought about how dishonest and disloyal he was being to Gun despite his scandalous ways. It wasn't his place to judge him. He repeated to Chen a number of times and then again often to his own reflection. Only now Terrence realized that his life as an assassin was a true double standard. He lived out his days paying unsuspecting souls visits to bring them to justice. The one he placed upon them, as he brought sorrow upon their families because of his sentencing them to death.

Truly Terrence was crying because of his own wrong doing. The guilt and pain ate away at his soul. In the back of his mind he admitted to his evil deeds and thought that whatever befell him he was deserving of it. After all, it was his judging others that would ultimately seal his fate. He wasn't God. He was playing a part due to the hurt and anger that he harvested in his heart. Gun played to that weakness and used Terrence to facilitate his madness by feeding the angry monster that lie dormant in Terrence's soul.

Chen grew even more anxious and ready for her standoff with Gun as she thought about all the people in her life he hurt. For all she knew he could have been behind her brother's mysterious suicide. She knew that he died from self-inflicted wounds but the feelings of abandonment were the weak spots that Chang-son wore on his sleeve. Had Gun had any recognition of this fact he would have played on it. She could see Gun convincing Chang-son that the only loyal thing to do to honor his father would be to take his own life. Chen shook her head visibly to chime back into reality. She was floating so far away there was no way she could have blocked the first blow from Gun's cowardice attack.

Gun smiled and snorted both sides of his nose and threw another punch towards Chen. That time she felt the anger behind his pummeling fists. She took it all in before she set-up ready to retaliate. Gun danced around happy to oblige her invitation.

"Now that's what I'm talking about." Gun was so excited he could hardly contain himself. Chen felt liberated as she licked the blood from her lips and threw her robe to the floor. Her apparent change of attire to pretend she was home all along hadn't panned out. Her red satin and black bra enticed Gun. He was ready to beat the living day light out of her and then fuck her brains out right there in the kitchen. Chen saw the uncertainty in

Gun's eyes and made her move. She went in hard and fast punching Gun as hard and fast as she could before landing a nice spin kick across his cheek and bottom lip with the heel of her black pumps.

Gun went down fast and hard. Chen's brow folded angry at his quick demise. She was just getting started and it felt good.

Gun sat on all fours looking towards the floor of the kitchen. Chen knew it was trouble. There was no way Gun was going to give up that easy whether they were alone or not. Chen was prepared to finish the job with or without Terrence.

"Look at you." Chen began her speech. Her chest was heaving in and out and her rib cage was visible. "Some gangsta you are," Chen threw on her black chick voice she liked to call it, as she bounced around like she was sparring. Chen thought she saw Gun motion for his knife so she ran up and kicked him in the face once more. Gun held his head low and spit the blood onto the floor. Angered by this, Chen threw a towel from the kitchen sink down onto the ground just in front of him and ordered him to clean up his mess.

"Bitch you have truly lost your mind." Gun picked up one of his legs and planted his foot firmly onto the ground. "I hope you plan to kill me Chen."

Chen smiled at his cockiness and demanded him to stand to his feet and look her in the face. She had retrieved her weapon and was waiting for Gun to make a move so she could splatter his brains all over the marble floors of their kitchen.

"Stand up!" Chen spoke softly and calm. She wanted him to know that she had all her senses and she was in no way under duress. Gun took offense to her calmness and wondered what or who had changed her composure. Gun's attention soon turned to this very fact. He paid little attention to Chen's demands at that point. He was more concerned about her new found confidence.

Chen's mind was shaky. Her hand trembled as her palms began to perspire. Her frustration was boiling over. She was beginning to have second thoughts about her confrontation with Gun. She didn't have the energy to fight with him any further. She was growing so tired of Gun dancing around the subject of her father, she started to just shoot him and get the whole ordeal over with.

"I loved you…, Gun you destroyed me and my life I gave up everything."

Gun looked at Chen as she spoke. "You are such a spoiled little brat…, always have been. You actually believe your own lies. You and I both know that your ass was born with a silver spoon. Your dad was the money." Gun was cunning and sarcastic as he began talking about Chen's father.

"Mr. Chang was a great leader he spoke with such conviction leading us to believe that we could have our cake and eat it too. The loyal and fair way right, treat everyone fairly, right? That shit wasn't true. Your father wasn't shit. He was a slave owner. He ordered us around to do is bid, just like every other public speaker. He was a motivational speaker nothing more, my friend. I did all the work. Those other numb nuts just followed the leader. Simon fucking says. Chen all the men were all greedy. They were stealing and collecting monies due your father under the fucking table, making deals with the Feds…., he was well on his way to jail Chen. We did him a favor. He died with honor. Not in some jail cell rotting away, or killed by some young thug with milk on his breath."

Chen was agitated. She couldn't believe Gun. His accusations were Ludacris. The fact that he said he had done her father a favor was the straw that broke the camel's back. She wanted to cut him wide open and watch him bleed to death.

"He died with honor, Chen."

"You are such a lying bastard. Yes, I'm sure dad's people were stealing. I am sure there were a few snitches lurking about; but I think the person with all these issues is standing right in front of me. It's just like you to blame everyone else but yourself. When are you going to stand up like a man and take responsibility for your own actions? This is so very pitiful. You indulged in this lifestyle. You are a greedy little man. When your desires weren't met I believe whole heartedly that you killed my father." Chen was yelling at the top of her lungs and spitting every syllable as she spoke. Chen waved the gun to and fro as she gave her speech about the men and Gun's deviant behavior.

"Is that right?"

Chen wasn't amused by Gun's lack of interest. "Out of all the people in my life, I never for a second thought it would be you. How could you kill my father?"

"Are you serious?" Gun lowered his eyes and motioned closer to Chen. "I didn't...The mob ordered the hit. Like I said before your father was involved in some very shady deals. You are so naive Chen, no wonder he never gave you any insight into his business. It wasn't because you were a woman. It was because he knew you were weak. Something I have been trying to cure in your fragile mind for years. Why this is the first time I have seen you stand up for yourself. Quite frankly, it turns me on."

Chen's lips pinched to a very thin line as she listened to the load of bull shit, Gun fed her. "Well Gun... I guess you are about to find out just how serious I am. I don't believe a word you are saying. The papers I found indicate you are the jealous one. Smitten for my Father's estate you were the one longing for a position at the head table. You used me as bait for each and every one of your hair brained schemes. Now I will carry their blood on my hands as well as yours.

"You don't have the balls to kill me." Gun straightened his posture, so he could stand tall and look his murderer in the face. "YOU THINK YOU CAN HURT ME CHEN? WELL... DO IT!" Gun began to yell at the top of his lungs instigating the fuels that burned Chen's anger to ignite.

"Shut....," Chen's throat caught an air bubble and for a second she choked on her words. "Shut-up," Chen started in again after clearing her throat. She was losing the upper hand with Gun.

"DO....IT," Gun shouted enunciating his words. He knew that his screaming intimidated her and it pleasured him to see her squirm. Chen swallowed hard and pulled the second gun from behind her back displaying just how in charge she was in the matter. The small 22 caliber automatic was tucked discreetly in the small of her back, seated just inside her panties.

Chen was serious in her endeavor, and knew that she had to complete the task or run the risk of death by her own weapon. Tears began to stream down Chen's face she was an emotional wreck realizing she was going to have to kill the love of her life. He was the man that had stood to the right of her Father for so many years. The same man however had been disloyal to the family an act punishable by death. The entire ordeal was taking its toll, an issue she had to profess in her private confessions.

Chen battled her conscience as Gun stood looking directly into the barrel of the gun with such a crazed look she couldn't be sure the bullet would penetrate his heart.

"What are you waiting for Chen? You've come this far."

Chen smiled. She spread her legs apart and rocked back and forth to exercise her legs. She was standing in her 3 inch heels and her calves burned. Of course Gun thought she was putting on a show for him, the self-indulgent bastard. She was sickened by his look of approval. His beady eyes were staring at her so intently she lost track of her mission a tad.

"I want you to confess to killing my Father. It's the least you can do. You contribute nothing to society. You are just taking up space. Why if I stayed with you I could never respect myself. Look at you sitting there breathing, as though you are worthy of air. The sight of you is repulsing." Chen drifted off as she began to take a trip down memory lane. One of her past memories she wished she could forget. Chen walked around the island of her kitchen pointing one of the guns directly at her husband's penis.

Chen shook her head and cursed Gun for his actions that beget hers. She knew that she would be no better than Gun if she went through with killing him; but it was about loyalty, respect, honor, and power that she hoped to reclaim.

"I was paralyzed from the waist down when I got the news, "Chen continued as she prepared to finish the job she started. Chen kept one of the guns fixated on her husband's limp dick as she pulled the kitchen drawer open to show off the documents she'd recovered from the safe in his office. Gun's penis was a flaccid as a deflated balloon when he realized that

Chen was aiming the Gun at his dick. His upper lip beaded with sweat.

"My eyes froze and had the reflection of a waterfall you remember don't you? You were there. I remember searching the faces of my father's men looking for clues. The tears I questioned to be true sincere. The all stood there with shocked mouths and wide eyes bewildered by the reality of their fallen leader. They judged one another based on their efforts to do their jobs. Those men blamed themselves because it was their duty to protect my father.

Gun adjusted his belt and snorted grossly as he turned up his nasty lips. His face was smug and his eyes seemed to darken.

"You know what? I never saw you shed a tear." Chen continued as she recollected the events of the day. She chuckled at how stupidly naive she had been. Shaking her head she closed her eyes briefly. "Back then I thought you were just being strong, that you were a strong leader, now I see your heart.

Gum grew so angry he was visibly red. "Your father was a COWARD!" Gun yelled into the face of Chen. He used the fact that I was in love with you to force me to do things I normally wouldn't. He left my family alone because I did what I had to do in order to keep him happy."

Chen was beginning to lose sight on the topic of the conversation .It seemed to be going South due to his suggestions of possible fornication. The secrets of the family seethed into Chen's skin and had begun to fester.

Chen's brother had committed suicide just 6 months prior to their father's passing. Talk about sexuality out of the norm was looked upon as socially inapt. The Chang family circle was close knit and secrets were forbidden especially those held by Chang-sun. Chen was visibly chiming in and out of consciousness as her mental state wavered. She was waving her gun and mumbling under her breath as if someone else was giving her orders. Chen put her hands to her face and patted the sweat from her brow. She was confused.

"What are you talking about Gun? My father was no coward, Gun."

Gun was both confused and afraid but he was alone. He couldn't be sure of Chen's agenda, though he knew that if given the slightest chance he would kill her in the most horrific way. It saddened him that Chen was oblivious to all the hurt and pain he suffered at the hands of her father. He had his reasons for ordering the hit, and it had nothing to do with money and power. He killed for survival. Mr. Chang had secrets himself, secrets that could ruin them both.

Like Chen, Gun's recollection of the past took him to a different land. He nearly threw up in his mouth at the thoughts of Mr. Chang's swollen sweaty palms fondling his private areas as a teen.

Mr. Chang was a nasty little man and he was his dirty little secret. Even in the face of death he couldn't bear to speak of the sadistic natures of Mr. Chang and his horrific childhood. He wouldn't dishonor himself or the image Chen held of her father. It was true that he wasn't a very good husband. He blamed Mr. Chang for this as well. He was angry at the happenings of the past and it soiled his love for Chen. Chen was his pride and joy but Mr. Chang's blood ran through her veins.

Chen interjected Gun's thoughts as she grew tired of Gun's pitiful mug. "Vengeance will be mine," Chen spoke as she wiped the paint from her eyes. She laughed as she recalled the look of fear in Gun's eyes when he read the notes yelling bloody murder. The murderous threats were just the beginning. The smell of gas spooked Gun so much he changed vehicles and drivers.

Chen kind of smirked as she thought about all the pranks she pulled to get Gun to believe the Korean mob was after him.

She cut the bushes in the lawn that covered the windows of Gun's office and left the window cracked to make it look like someone had intruded the home.

When Gun awoke that morning and went to his office he found a large hole in the form of a grave dug out on the front lawn; with a fake tombstone that read his name. Gun was frantic. He ran about the home checking all the doors and windows, and demanded to see all the surveillance tapes for the entire week. Nothing out of the ordinary was ever found, which made Gun an angry and demented boy.

For some reason the incident hadn't been recorded. Gun blamed his med and thought for sure he had a traitor on his hands. He became obsessed with getting to the bottom of the grave and cut bushes. He stuck to Terrence like glue. He figured he was the only person he could trust. Gun was right. It was an inside job and the closet to his person was responsible.

Chen was smiling unwaveringly. "The look on your face was priceless. You can wipe that smug look from your lips."

Chen motioned Gun to take a seat in the chair she had out in the middle of the marble floor in the living room. The room was dark and empty after her staged robbery, another one of Chen's dirty deeds.

The robbery wasn't a robbery at all. She simply had her furniture moved to her new upscale apartment in Long Beach. Terrence had been left out of that plot due to his latest snobbery. She wasn't sure of his faithfulness to her alliance.

Gun was impressed as he listened to Chen confess her part in his demise. He was excited by her undercover operatives. He was in love with her this he knew. He just couldn't be sure he was looking at Chen or the doing of another lover that had brain washed and turned her against him.

Even still, he had to admit that he was obliged to shake the man's hand that could turn sweet and innocent Chen to the, "Bonnie," he had always longed for, another one of his favorite duos in the land of gangs and organized crime, "Bonnie and Clyde."

Gun clapped vigorously as he smiled at Chen for her success in undercover operations. He wanted desperately to take her into his arms and have sex with her before he strangled her as they both climaxed.

Chen wasn't amused. She was waiting for her confession and she didn't care what Gun had to say on any of the matters that had taken place leading up to her moment of peace and tranquility.

"Now confess…" Chen motioned her gun to a side position as if she were a gangster straight out of Compton. She stood tall in her black and red stilettos waiting for him to buck.

Gun lowered his eyes, and for a second thought about testing just how brassy Chen's nuts were. She was so beautiful to him he could feel his love rise just as his anger. He couldn't wait to taste her blood. He could see the fire in her eyes. He only wished she had been such a ride or die bitch in Korea. The visions of, "Scarface," made him smile. It was his favorite depiction of what he claimed to be his model life. Gun chuckled a bit and looked directly into Chen's eyes.

"No Because I am not the one who murdered your Father. I ordered the hit." Gun danced around a bit as he played with the blade of his knife. He was cutting himself purposely as he slid his thumb across the sharp edge, sucking the blood from his wounds.

"So what now...," Gun looked up from his self-mutilation and shrugged his shoulders. "I guess I did kill your father theoretically, but I'm not the one that slit his throat.

Chen's mouth dropped as she fell into the very emotions she was trying so hard to hide. Her tears became that of a tantrum. Gun simply laughed at her emotional display. He was winning and he loved to see just how weak she was. Chen didn't know what to do. She was flabbergasted at how nonchalant and conniving Gun was. If he was so big and bad the least he could do was admit to his transgressions and die with honor.

Gun looked down at his hands and flexed his chest.

"You know Chen I am growing very impatient by your ridiculous display. Let's either get this over with, or I we can go up to our room and we can forget this little escapade ever happened."

Chen knew that such an act would never be forgotten or forgiven. He would be sure to kill her in her sleep, but not before he raped her over and over again both physically and mentally.

Chen's knees began to grow weak and she was faltering in her decision to kill Gun. Perhaps if she contacted the authority's they would just come and get him. Lock him up for life and save them both from such an agony of pain. She knew that if she pulled the trigger she would have to live with her acts for the rest of her life, and she wasn't sure she could any more.

Gun looked up from his moment of meditation and pulled his knife from his back pocket. He was thinking that while she was contemplating her latest actions he could overpower her quite easily with a puncture straight through her arm. He didn't want to kill her right away. He wanted to taste her sweet juices just one more time before sending her to hell.

"Chen, what the fuck are you doing?" Terrence galloped in as though he were riding a white horse and demanded an explanation from Chen. She was already getting nervous about shooting Gun, and with him towards the back of her she thought she had lost the battle. Terrence stood still as he too went over his rules of camaraderie. His loyalty had changed during the course of his stay with Chen; but he wasn't sure Chen loved him the way he hoped, especially after she'd drugged him the night before.

Gun looked up from his playful toying with his machete somewhat bummed about his recue.

"Man…, where have you been? Get this bitch from my sight before I am forced to kill her." Gun bit his bottom lip and flexed his muscles as if he had grown an extra set of balls in the last few seconds. Big Terrence had come to his rescue. His voice had a few added decimals in bass and his swag was filled with arrogance. He was king and Chen would now pay for her disloyalty to the family. Gun took a moment to collect his thoughts. He ventured over to the sink and wet a paper towel to clean his wounds.

Chen didn't say a word. She was waiting to see what Terrence's next move would be. She was ready for whatever. Her heart had been broken several times so she was beginning to get used to abandonment.

Chen finally turned her attention to Terrence she had yet to deter from Gun. She could care less he entered into the room, as long as he had her back.

"Terrence… don't be stupid. I am going to follow through with this. He murdered my father and if we ever want to be together you know it has to be done. If I don't kill him now he will surely kill us both. He is nothing Terrence. I am the one with all the money."

Gun looked in surprise about the words that were falling from Chen's mouth.

"She right about that Bro…, she got the doe. So she say…, but I know you riding with me, "Big T," Bro's before Hoe's right dog?" Gun was confident in his loyal friend. He was on a rampage eager to give Chen the business. Gun turned his attention to Chen.

"Boy are you as stupid as they come. Your father was right about your senses. They are indeed incredibly short. I don't think you understand the situation, Chen." Gun lowered his eyes and looked at Terrence with such fire, Chen's cheeks warmed. He rubbed his chin with his wet palms in an effort to cool down the fires brewing deep in his soul. He couldn't believe Chen's accusations. Convinced he had to have heard Chen's admission of fornication he again directed his attention to Terrence.

"TERRENCE…" Gun yelled growing both agitated and worried. "What's taking you so long to shoot Chen? I'm sorry do you not see that she has a gun drawn on your boss?" Gun began to laugh hysterically at how deranged Chen had become. Her eyes were wide and bouncing back and forth from the two men frantically.

Chen's lips began to quiver as she became confused about the two men standing before her. She needed to think fast, before she too was staring down the barrel of a smoking gun.

"Terrence did you get the bags?" Chen looked at Terrence nervously. She knew full well he had no idea of her inquiry but she had to find out if he was two seconds from pouncing on her as well. She needed to know that he was still on her side, and the only way to do that was to literally throw him under the bus to bring light to their affair.

Gun licked his lips and spit directly on the floor in anger and disgust.

"You bitch ass mother fucker," Gun's Asian accent had a hint of urban flavor to it so that Terrence could get the full understanding of his mission. "I am going to kill you, you fucking my wife, Terrence?"

Terrence instantly stepped forward and took his place in front of Chen. He eyeballed Gun with the most cunning look of rage. Gun questioned his authority. Terrence was forced to honor his heart.

"Yes, that's right," Terrence admitted and folded his arms, flexing his muscles.

Gun's eyes began to water. He closed them tightly to erase the presence of weakness.

A i j a   M .

"Chen is this true?" Gun looked around Terrence's burly physique and froze on Chen's face. He looked into Chen's eyes waiting for confirmation.

"It's true...so why don't you just confess to murdering my father so I can get this show on the road. I think we have had enough fun for tonight." Chen looked around and wobbled a bit. She was growing tired of her Bad Bitch attire. She was ready to dress down and dig into a half gallon of ice cream. Her standing up to Gun alone was a step towards independence in itself, which is why she questioned the need to kill him. Gun may have killed her father but it didn't give her the right to take matters into her own hands. She wanted to honor her father, and bringing Gun to justice would pay homage. Only she didn't have the evidence she needed. There was no weapon. The only proof she had were insurance policies and her father's necklace he wore so proudly.

"Well Chen I guess you get a two for one special tonight, huh? You get the guy that ordered the hit on your father and the man who actually pulled the trigger or gut his ass shall I say?" Gun hunched up his shoulders and gave a look to Chen that said my bad I didn't mean to say that. He was sarcastic and cunning. The look on Chen's face was worth the bullet.

Uncertain of what Gun suggested Chen turned her attention to Terrence. His face was solemn but stern. Chen could tell that Gun's accusations were true by the look in Terrence's eyes. Chen was devastated about the news. She nearly dropped the gun to the floor as she searched Terrence's eyes for the truth. A truth Terrence vowed to take to his grave for fear of losing Chen.

"It was a job, Chen."

Showdown... Chen couldn't believe her

ears. She chuckled in disbelief and shook her head as she couldn't believe how nonchalant Terrence was being in regards to the murder of her father. After all this time she spent with him planning Gun's demise, not one time had she considered Terrence's possible participation in the plot to kill her father. But then again, why not, he was loyal to Gun. His only argument during their time of lust and revenge was the fact that he stood by Gun so many years. Terrence noted quite often how bad he felt about betraying Gun. Never had he had the inclination that perhaps her reason for killing Gun was warranted.

He didn't care to hear much of her story as she recalled. Chen was still standing but she could feel herself hit the floor as her heart broke. Terrence looked remorseful; but his eyes told a different story. One that couldn't let him truly love Chen because those demons he had fought so hard to subdue were resurfacing in that very moment. Now Terrence wasn't sure he ever had feelings for Chen. He wasn't sure if he was all part of her mission to do away with Gun so that she could live her life freely without consequences.

The funny thing is there was no life without consequences, responsibility, or independence.

"Shi..., you can believe that croak if you want to," Terrence was shaking his head and talking under his breath but Chen caught his words and demanded an explanation. Terrence didn't respond as he felt he didn't have to. The fact of the matter was he too had a valid argument. He was betrayed as well. By Chen herself, she drugged him because she wasn't trusting of him. That very fact told Terrence that what Chen felt for him couldn't be true.

Chen's vision was spotty as her eyes watered and her nose began to run slightly. She was so hurt she could barely stand. Chen took a seat in the chair she placed out for Gun's confession and put her head in her hands. She closed herself tightly trying desperately to disappear from the situation without being noticed. Gun was amused.

"What...you thought Terrence loved you or something?" Gun was prancing around her chair like he was playing musical chairs and mimicking, "Kat William's," stage presence.

"Yeah I did actually," Chen stood up hard and fast and hit Gun over the head with the butt of her gun as he walked around her chair for the last time. He had aggravated her to the point of no return. She obviously didn't need a fucking confession because the man she had fallen for slit her father's throat.

"Chen let's go! I am sorry..., what I did happened it was a job, and at the time I didn't know who he was to you. "

Terrence was telling the truth on that part. He was Gun's boy. He knew of Mr. Chang and his dealings, but he never had any direct contact with him and his family. Gun was the affiliate of the Chang family and he got his points from sleeping with Mr. Chang on the low. It was a horrible price he paid to squash the debt his father had. He owed the Chang family a substantial amount of cash. After the cops got whiff of the drugs and illegal selling of teen girls, cops ransacked the club and ceased all assets.

Gun and his family became a direct target. Mr. Chang could care less about the circumstances. He was out of well over 3 million dollars in cash not to mention the coke.

Chen's father was merely a task. Gun promised Terrence riches he knew he couldn't otherwise afford. That was the only motive he needed. Falling for Chen was never in the cards. After all he was Gun's bodyguard. Loyalty had always been on top of Terrence's list in any regard to the job aside from the money and power.

Chen's mouth was so pinched with disgust her lips were but a mere line. She didn't know where she would throw up or commence to firing her weapon at whatever moved in her circumference. Terrence felt like crying. Gun was busy sharpening his knife as if he had complete control of the situation, while Chen couldn't decide who she was going to shoot first.

"Let's go, Chen," Terrence demanded once more.

"Nigga are you crazy?" Gun budded in as if he was dumbfounded at how ignorant Terrence was acting in the whole matter. "I am going to give the two of a head start before I kill the both of you traitors. If you don't…get…your….shit, and get the fuck out of…my…home. I am going to slit your throats. This has all been quite an eye opening eve for me and I would just like to get some rest." Gun shook his head as he paused for a brief moment to look into the faces of both Chen and Terrence. "Ain't this about a Bitch? Be sure to take out the trash, and by that I mean you Chen. You can have the dirty slut. They're plenty out her in good ole California, isn't that right Terrence?"

By then, Gun was prancing around raising and slicing the wind with his blade as though he was drunk and his motor

82 | P a g e
B u t l e r
A i j a M .

skills were diminishing. Terrence stood at attention and had no desire to give Gun an explanation or respond to his threats. Gun knew full well he could take him down if he desired. Chen was the one he was worried about. He honestly didn't want Gun's blood on her hands.

Terrence stepped in front of Chen to make sure she didn't fire her weapon. She was reluctant to trust Terrence but she knew that he their times together were real. Though she still questioned how far their lustful passions could go. Was the affair just that or had it transpired into a relationship that the two of them could quite possibly build on? Terrence had to understand that her reasoning for drugging him were not to deceive him but to protect him.

Gun wasn't amused at the small meeting Chen and Terrence were having. He licked the butt of his knife and gritted his teeth.

"AH….." Gun lunged at Terrence stabbing him over and over in the back. Terrence's eyes grew wide as he starred back at Chen.

Chen stepped back and fired her weapon piercing Gun in his right shoulder first. Her adrenaline level seemed to rise at the sight of his blood. His eyes turned a deep black. He looked like a crazed animal, some what possessed even.

Gun was stabbing Terrence in any orifice he could reach. Terrence fell into Chen before falling to the floor. Chen fired her weapon once more and then again. Gun toppled to the floor after hitting his head on the edge of the nook in the kitchen. Chen's hands burned and her eyes were itching from the sweat dancing down the sides of her eyebrows. She anxiously took her place over Gun's head. She placed one leg across his head so that her vagina was in full view. She wanted to go give him one last peak before she sealed his fate.

Even in death his crude idea of passion and romance was horrifically exhibited. Gun licked his lips and flicked his tongue at the exhibition of Chen's opening.

"Let me taste it one last time." Gun spit out gurgling blood.

Chen was so angry flashes of Gun raping her over and over again ran and sped towards the beatings and public humiliation over the years. The jolt of the gun firing in such close range sent Gun's blood up into the air. Chen caught some of it on her lip and she took every satisfaction licking her lips as she watched Gun exhale for the last time.

Chen was standing lost in translation watching Gun. She wanted to make sure that his chest had ceased to rise and fall. In the back of her mind she could hear Terrence calling out to her but she couldn't take her eyes off of Gun.

Terrence could feel his life slipping away. He took every ounce of strength left in him and screamed for Chen to call 911.

"Chen…," Terrence fought his urge to pass out as he called out to her.

Like a light switch came on inside Chen's head she quickly removed her shoes and ran to Terrence's side. Chen grabbed for the phone and called for assistance. It was then that Terrence closed his eyes and past out cold in the fold of Chen's arms.

Flashing lights were all Terrence could see as he fell in and out of consciousness. Chen was sitting at his side. She was blood soaked. The medics had tried several times to clean her up, but she refused. Gun's blood was on her hands and so was Terrence's. She wasn't ready to let go of either one of them just yet. She was still reeling over her new found confidence to stand up to the beast. She was happy she killed him. Though Terrence pushed her to step in, she found the strength to fight for what she loved.

The fear still remained that a life of crime would soon catch up to her. Even though she wasn't the direct facilitator of the madness, she was his wife. Those looking for Gun could very well come for her. She wanted to seek peace on earth for herself. She couldn't be sure Terrence could provide the safe haven she sought either. His tense exterior is beyond rough on the edges. The breakthrough was a teeter tottering slope.

Terrence was taken right into surgery as soon as they arrived at the hospital. It wasn't until questioned that Chen seemed to awake from a dream and her mental state started to normalize. Police were more interested in the company Gun kept and the paper trail linking him to many gambling forums and organized crime units. The fact that she shot him was immediately ruled as an act of self-defense.

Terrence was still in very critical condition however. She was worried that he wouldn't survive the attack. Chen cooperated with the police as best as she could stomach before returning to the admission desk at the hospital. It was going to be a few hours at least before Terrence were out of surgery so she decided to go back home and collect the remainder of her things. She wanted to get as far away as possible from the house she for 3 years called home.

Fear was no longer a factor in her life. She could make her own decisions. Chen thought about Terrence and her feelings for him. She was sure that what they shared was more than a fling, but she wasn't sure that they could truly build on their sexual escapades. Then there was the issue of her father's murder. She realized that he was just a hit on his long list of victims; but the fact remained that he was her father. Chen was so confused. She didn't know if she could look into the face of a man that murdered her father. Then to separate himself from any human emotion and state out loud that he was nothing but a job; caused Chen to question his ability to love.

Chen walked slowly towards the exit doors of the hospital. As she drew closer to the doors the tears began to flow.

"Ma'am…" One of the nurses tried to flag down Chen as she left the building. She wanted to see about her signing some of the permission slips needed in case of emergencies and such.

Chen lost her place on earth. Her mind flashed back to a place of darkness, as she was sure they were calling to arrest her for Gun's murder. In the blink of an eye Chen found herself back in her home under the confines of rules and regulations, shielding herself from Gun's blows.

Fearing for her safety and unwillingness to surrender to Gun's wrath, Chen ran from the hospital and out into the parking lot in search for a cab. She was distraught and out of her mind. Chen had slipped into a state of shock. She'd just murdered her husband; but she was sure he would haunt and kill her. Chen was so afraid for her life she didn't stop to look back. She ran 6 blocks straight before stopping at a stoop for a breath of air. Her feet were raw and bloody just as her hands. She was wearing hospital scrubs that were baggy on her waist.

Chen hailed for a cab. She was weary and dizzy from her sprint and just wanted to lay down in the backseat and enjoy her ride to freedom. The cab driver was a nasty bugger. He drove like a bat out of hell. Her stomach was worse than ever. The yelling didn't calm her whirlwind of terror either, she was sure she was going to vomit all over the backseat of Mr. Morrison's cab. Just as he continued to warn her about the cleaning fee she would be subjected to had she grown sick in the back of his cab?

Mr. Morrison's cab identification card was her focus. It was the only thing she could see. The cab drivers name tag was flapping in the wind as they turned the corner to her street. She nearly missed her stop.

"Twenty bucks," Mr. Dick yelled back without turning his head. He was happy to rid himself of a possible law suit. He didn't want to have a sick or dead girl on his hands.

Chen searched her bra; all she had was two, two hundred dollar bills. Without a second thought she just threw one of the bills his way and slithered out of the cab. She needed to get to the bathroom and fast.

Chen wasn't two steps into her front gate before she vomited all over the lawn. She was so dizzy and out of breath she thought she would need a medic. She was dehydrated and weak in the knees. Her feet were swollen from standing in her heels for just over 3 hours and her arms were sore. She could barely put her key into the door.

Once Chen was inside she retreated up to her master bedroom she locked the door behind her and went to draw herself a bath. She wanted to wash the blood and stink from her soul in hopes for redemption. Chen didn't bother waiting on the tub to fill she shed her clothing and jumped into the tub to await the cleansing process.

Chen soaked for about an hour outlining her next plan of action. Her sense of peace was overshadowed however by the uncertainty of Terrence's condition. She loved him. She also hated him. It took everything in her not to reach across and slit his throat as he called for help.

Chen called herself to those moments before her conscious would allow her to react to Terrence's plight. She wanted him to die as well. She just couldn't bring herself to kill him. It was about honor and respect. Clearly he was obedient; but he had taken a life that meant the world to her.

Chen thought about how much she revealed to Terrence. She bore her soul. Still, he never shared with her the contents of his heart except for his brother's death. Even then he left out emotion. He looked on to life as a job. He wasn't able to live for the guilt he held with in his soul. His mission was revenge. Chen had to admit that in the last few years of her life she sought the same.

Chen closed her eyes and sunk down to the bottom of the tub. She emerged herself completely under the bubbles and held her breath for as long as she could. Sightings of the two men she once loved flashed before her eyes. The nightmares began in broad day. Gun was stabbing her and Terrence was strangling the life she struggled to hold on to. Chen scrambled about the tub fighting to escape from under Terrence's hold. He was holding her down as she frantically tried to flee the sharp object Gun plunged into her flesh over and over again.

The jolt of her belly danced and butterflies emerged to the top of the blood thickened water as she floated slowly towards the top of the tubs edge.

Chen's eyes burst open having had an epitome.

"Oh my God…, I'm pregnant."

Victim of

Circumstance... Terrence opened his eyes

and followed the drips from his IV down the tube of his injection sight. He listened intently at his monitors beeping sounds. He made an attempt to raise his head to get a glimpse of his surroundings. The police weren't present. That was a good sign so Terrence rested his head on his stiff white pillow and pushed his nurse call button. His throat was parched. He was also alone and he feared for his safety. His life as a bounty hunter and assassin was a dangerous one. His "*John Doe*," status was a Godsend.

Terrence took a few breaths to test out how serious his condition was. It hurt like hell, he decided; but he had to laugh at how ride or die Chen had been. She was blasting away at Gun. The sight was vicious and a turn on just the same.

"How are you feeling today? You gave us quite a scare." The nurse on call came around the corner to check on Terrence's vital signs. As she checked the flow of his IV, Terrence reached over and grabbed the woman's wrist.

"I need a phone." Terrence's raspy voice was shackled by a splintering pain that caught his open pores as his lips parted. His lips were chapped they burned as he spoke.

"Why don't we get your meds going and some food in your system before we start making phone calls? What do you say?"

Terrence wasn't happy but he had to admit the pain was catching onto his nerves in a major way. "Sure ok, sounds good."

"Okay, I will be right back."

"A...," Terrence blurted before the nurse could fully leave his presence. He was desperate to find out if Chen had been there to see him or if she was perhaps still around the hospital. Sadly, he refrained as the nurse turned to respond to his inquiry. "Never mind...," Terrence decided it best to keep his wishes to himself for fear his emotions would take him under.

Terrence guzzled down about four 16oz cartons of milk and a pitcher of water, yet somehow he was still thirsty. He was nervous. Chen had yet to call or show face. What could be taking her so long? Terrence felt a ball rising in his throat that stifled his breathing.

The take was his interest. She owed him well over a million dollars for agreeing to her devious plot to get rid of Gun. He reckoned she wouldn't run. He was a firm believer in the power of the pipe. He trusted that his long stroke stuck to her hormones like a wet dream. He fell only so far. He did agree that he owed her a free fuck for saving his life; but money was money.

"It was just a job," Terrence uttered to himself.

Terrence was no fool. As fast as that girl's panties got wet so did appear her green eyes. She was as greedy as Gun. She however came with just the right goods of service that could make any man lie down.

****

Chen jumped from bed and rushed to get dressed. She was excited about the news. Terrence was awake but more than that she had an appointment, to prove her premonition of pregnancy.

Chen slid on a sleek fitting black mini skirt and low button satin blouse. She starred at her reflection in the mirror. Her makeup was flawless. Her hair had a new shine and her curls fell into place. Though her stage presence was on point her mind was in disarray. She was elated at the possibility of pregnancy; but worried that Terrence would find out and come after her about the paternity of her child. She couldn't allow that to happen. The best thing for her to do would be to pay Terrence and get a move on. His lifestyle was in no way fitting for a child or a wife for that matter. The one thing they did share besides the sheets was their selfish ways. They were too busy plotting to get Gun; they hadn't bothered to consider the consequences of sex without protection.

Chen's infatuation with her new found glow was ended by the burn and stabbing taking place in her womb. She grabbed quickly at her pelvis as the pain swirled from left to right. The twinge culminated smack dab in the pit of her stomach. The growth was pulsating and heaving life an infestation coming to a head.

The sudden vicious strike made Chen call out in agony. She fell towards the sink and grabbed about her vanity area in search of something to relieve the pain. Her doctor's appointment couldn't have come.at a better time. Chen was worried and weary. She didn't want to drive at that point, but she wanted to make sure her life and the life of her baby was ok.

As the pain hit home so did the realities of her present life. The life she vowed to take back. She had a fresh start. If she forced a life with Terrence she would be spending most of her days trying to crack the code behind his life of anger and crime. It would ultimately take away from her child. She couldn't be sure that the baby was even his, her gut couldn't tell the difference either.

Chen's stomach turned as her thoughts ran towards having Guns child. His heart was rotten. Gun was a victim of circumstance and so was she. Her father played a horrible role and perhaps his death was his justice. Chen recalled her father's rule of thumb. He lied once again to her and to his followers. His concept of fairness may have been true; but he was nothing but a cruel greedy man. He stole Gun's innocence. His thoughts behind treating others fairly and choosing ones sword could have been true. Only, the sword he secretly chose was a malicious one and so he died by it.

Chen sat down on top of her toilet seat and twiddled her thumbs. She looked down on to the Pergo flooring and studied its pattern. The faces of all three men that had played a part in her disheveled life rippled across the diamond patterns. The vision clearly shook her. All she could see was blood, murder, and screaming women trying to flee the scene. Most of her life she was that woman. To Chen, it was a message to her directly from her Father.

Terrence had been a tool she used when she needed to feel love or she needed things done. She knew in her heart of hearts she couldn't trust him for the long haul. After all, he was Guns right hand man. Loyalty to Terrence was very important to him.

Chen made a few calls after she dealt with the demons of her conscience. It was time to go. The apartment in Long Beach was situated and her plane tickets and time of flight was confirmed. Chen wrote out a check to Terrence in the amount of 2 million dollars and slipped it into her purse. She swallowed two pills and checked her make-up one last time before slipping on her pumps. She couldn't wait to get out of California. She had, had enough of the fast life. Terrence couldn't know of her pregnancy either, she couldn't let the lifestyle float into another generation.

The Chang legacy would end with her. She had put an end to Gun's reign and honored her father. His sins were his own. She too, may be called to pay the debts of her sins; but it won't be by the use of her children. Her son or daughter will never know of the happenings of her childhood or marriage with Gun. This was something she would take to her grave.

Chen buckled her seat belt and took a look at her reflection in the mirror and smiled. She was leaving everything behind. She had no desires to travel with baggage. She had her money all she needed to ensure was her health.

Chen sped away with the wind in her hair. "One last stop and I am home free," Chen whispered as she floated on cloud nine.

Terrence was sleeping when she walked into the room but the fragrance of her perfume caught his senses. He stirred slightly and whispered her name. It sent chills down Chen's spine but she held on to her stern look. She didn't want to show any signs of emotion. Her skin had more color and her breast for fuller. It was something Terrence caught on to right away. He hadn't been hospitalized 72 hours and her entire persona had changed. She was radiant.

Chen smiled when she noticed Terrence had opened his eyes to greet her. He looked horribly malnourished. Chen was shaky because she knew the excitement of a child and new life was hard for her to contain. Especially with someone she had spent the last few months with sharing her most intimate secrets and past experiences with.

Still, Chen had to stick to her guns about keeping her life change to herself. She would ensure Terrence received payment and be on her way. Terrence would be fine. He always had been. He just needed to work out the evils in his life.

There was no way she could risk the healing of her own wounds and the clean slate her and her child had to wallow in self-pity along with Terrence.

"So, Terrence looked into Chen's eyes with a look of pain and excitement all balled into one. Chen secretly wished that he showed sincere interest in their relationship but it became clear that he was waiting on payment for his services.

"I have the check." Chen looked up as she slipped the folded check from her purse. She slowly walked over to Terrence and placed it in his hand.

Terrence looked slightly shocked and saddened about the end events of their relationship but the feel of the check made his loins ache for something fruity with an umbrella dancing in its sweet intoxicating juices. He was planning on getting the hell out of dodge himself. He had, had enough of the life. At least until he was in full recovery. He was hanging up his leather bomber for a pair of shorts and wife beater. Terrence wiggled his toes as he thought of the sand playfully tickling his feet, as he unfolded the check for review.

"If that is all…," Chen interjected. She was serious and ready to go. She decided that her affair was just that and it there was no need for explanation. The job was done.

Terrence cleared his throat and tried to put some effort into sitting up to give her a proper goodbye but he was too weak. His wounds were still very raw and with one sudden move he would surely tear his stitching.

Chen saw his struggles and quickly put her hand up. "It's ok, don't get up. Take care."

"Where are you off to?" Terrence asked for more reason than he would like to admit. He didn't want to appear like a complete asshole. A feeling he had to get used to. His emotions were starting to override reason.

"Home, I have some packing to do. I want to get out of that house as fast as I can and into my own space. I'm just ready to start over you know…"

"I concur." Terrence let out an over exaggerated fake yawn, one Chen caught on to rather quickly.

Chen laughed out loud at Terrence's deliberate attempt to get rid of her. "Well good day," Chen smiled. "Oh and Terrence…"

"Yeah," Terrence responded in his sickly voice.

"You don't have to front with me. I know the deal. It's just a job right? It's all about the money." Chen didn't wait for a response. She turned on her heel and sped down the corridors of the intensive care unit and right out the doors of the hospital. Shaking her head as the wind danced in her curls.

ONE WEEK LATER

Checkmate... "Looking good..., looking good...Terrence." You all set and ready to go?"

"Oh yes partner an island awaits. I think I may try my hand at cooking some Caribbean foods Mon," Terrence added in his ghetto Jamaican voice. He was ready to get a move on. The week he spent in the hospital recuperating seemed like a month. It did give him some time to think about what he wanted out of life.

Life in the fast lane wasn't at all his choice of lifestyle. He lived it and survived; but he was in search for comfort. The check in his pocket was on fire. Terrence couldn't wait to get to his bank and put the money into his account. He had a number of loose ends to tie up before getting on the first thing smoking to New York. From there he would board the ship to Jamaica. Terrence closed his eyes and inhaled as if he smelled the cool winds of the island.

"You all right bro...," Terrence's driver thought maybe Terrence had lost his swag for a moment. "I hope this stabbing hasn't made a Bitch out you, my man."

"Never...," Terrence growled as his close friend and driver lowered his eyes. He was searching Terrence's countenance to make sure he was still the same as before.

"I'm cool bro don't worry. Now, get me out of here. I need to pick my car up from storage. I appreciate you coming to get me."

"So....,"

"Don't ask, don't even ask. She was a job. Its best we leave all that mambo jumbo to the streets, you feel me? I think this whole ordeal has changed my outlook on things."

"Oh yeah…"

"Yeah…now roll me out of here. I think if I see one more needle I may cry." Terrence plopped down into his wheel chair ready for his escort to wheel him to freedom.

Terrence's driver spun him around and headed down the hall. As a ritual and farewell the nurses of the wing stood out and clapped for his recovery. Terrence smiled a little, before asking everyone to quiet down so that he could make his exit speech. He was cocky as hell but the ladies loved it.

"So…thanks for having me." Terrence said as he chuckled. "If you ever need some help in the kitchen look me up. The food here is bland as hell." Terrence started to laugh incredibly hard. Too hard in fact, he nearly burst one of his stitches near his back. Terrence felt like a regular person. The murders of his past were crimes committed by someone else. He had a fresh start, a two million dollar fresh start.

Terrence and his driver rolled out of the hospital and into the busy streets of Los Angeles. He got into the car with very little assistance and his heart rate began to normalize. He was free. He couldn't help but think about Chen. How she might be doing or what she was up to. The fact was that the two together were poison. It was best they parted company. He wished her the best.

Terrence and his driver rolled up to a secluded garage where he held his belongings. He needed to grab a few bags for his travels and of course one of his whips. He knew that Malcolm would look after his prized possessions. He had to admit he wasn't too worried about his past riches. The items he accumulated were constant reminders of his anger and kills. He wanted a fresh start. The fresh start he couldn't wait to get to the bank and cash in on.

Terrence pulled down the door to his storage unit with a slight wince of pain. He growled below his breath but it was loud enough for Malcolm to catch wind of it.

"You alright, I thought I heard a Bitch scream." Malcolm chuckled. Terrence turned around and flared his nose a bit.

Malcolm put up his hands in a show of submission. "I'm just kidding."

"Yeah ok," Terrence responded. Terrence rolled his duffle to the trunk of his car and threw it in. He was excited to get on with his life. His bouts in Korea he just assumed died with Gun. He was glad that he was the invisible black knight. He was Gun's right hand but he was invisible to his hunts. Knowing this, he could close his eyes peacefully at night.

Terrence gave Malcolm a nice slap in the hand and jumped into his ride. He was about fifteen minutes from the bank and about an hour and half away from his flight out to New York. Terrence threw on his shades, popped his collar, and put the petal to the metal. He was on a time schedule and he needed about three hundred thousand dollars to get him started in the islands. His only hope was that the bank teller wouldn't pussy foot about getting his money together. It was something about Black men collecting money that made white feet slither.

The drive to the bank was a blur. It was just as well. His thoughts ran poorly towards the cream of Chen's thighs. He could have sworn he heard her voice call out to him twice as he drove down the highway. It wasn't a good look. Him salivating over a broad that didn't belong to him, she was a damn job.

Terrence's palms were sweating like he was planning to rob the joint. He was standing in line flicking his check back and forth. He read it over and over again making sure that his name was spelled correctly and all the zeros were present. He couldn't believe he had cashed in on such a sweet deal. Chen was worth far more than the two measly million bucks she doled his way. It was more than he'd been accustomed to, so beggars can't be choosers. It was a big job. He earned every penny. The sex was the perk. Oh how good it was. She could make him cum from just the looks of her wetness.

Terrence was getting too happy as he floated pornographic images across his mind. His love was rising and he was growing uncomfortable.

"Sir, can I be of assistance to you?"

"Uh yes, I would like to deposit this check and see about getting some cash for my trip."

"Ok sir, how much cash are we looking at today? How much is the check?"

"Two million and I need about three hundred thousand."

The teller raised one eyebrow as she looked over her glasses. She was checking his nationality he was sure of it. "Well now, with such a large amount of cash I am sure you understand we will have to verify this check before we could disperse any cash."

Terrence was hot under the collar almost immediately. His dick went limp and his attitude changed. The bones in Terrence's jaw were now visible.

"How long will that take ma'am…," Terrence spoke through clenched teeth?

"Well…if the check clears no time at all. If you would just have a seat over in our accounts area I will look up the account on which the check is drawn and make sure the funds are available, I will be back in a jiffy."

"Ok…" Terrence tapped on the counter of the teller's window and took a seat directly across from her station so that he could watch the facial expressions of the workers that were checking on his money. Terrence was anxious. He constantly checked the time on his watch. He didn't want to miss his plane. Terrence noticed two of the workers stationed behind the bullet proof glass giving him the eye as he checked his watch. He decided that perhaps he looked suspicious so he refrained from checking the time any further. Instead he took to watching the clock on the wall every five seconds.

After a long fifteen minute wait the teller came back from the office and called Terrence to the window. Terrence was happy because the look on the woman's face didn't indicate that she had run into problems.

"So what's the deal?" Terrence bounced up to the window excited about his two million dollar come up.

"Why Terrence that's the exact question I was about to ask you." The lady smiled at Terrence with delight. She was excited to catch herself a fraudulent varmint at her window and she was determined to make a spectacle of her find.

"What the fuck are you talking about?" Terrence was not amused one bit. He wanted his cash and he wanted it now. "Look lady I don't have time for your games. Can we just get the verification process over and done with so I can get my cash and be on my way?"

"How about you just be on your way, there is no money, no Chen Chang, and this here check is drawn on an account that has been closed for at least 6 months. "

Terrence's face broke and fell to pieces. He was sure he would shed a tear. The teller was talking, blabbering on about Chen's name and how funny it was. She had no sensitivity in the matter. There he stood holding his dick and the Bitch was probably half way around the world by now. Terrence was fuming. His first thought was to drive straight to Chen's Long Beach apartment and strangle the shit out of her. He knew better than that though, she was long gone.

"That dirty Bitch," Terrence spoke a loud biting his bottom lip.

"Excuse me sir, what did you say to me?"

"I said fuck you," Terrence said in almost a low growl as he spun around and walked out the bank.

"It's cool Chen…I'll catch you in your sleep. I will be sure to catch you while you sleep."

Author Aija M. Butler

Author *Aija Monique Butler*, was born in San Diego California, in 1979. She currently resides in the San Francisco Bay area. She is a Residential Care Facility Administrator for the State of California, Specializing in Acute Care, Dementia, and Diabetes, for the elderly.

She is an Advocate and Philanthropist for non-profit program development in the areas of Youth and Social Service Development. She is a grant writer and has an academic background in psychology and medicine. *Aija* has a love for the arts and is a writer of poetry, both fiction, and non-fiction novels, memoirs, and screen plays.

In 2012 Aija Butler, became the founder and executive director of, "Dis Me, The Blog Diary's," A Literary group which looks to help students learn how to use effective communication in expressing thoughts and feelings with their peers and elders. This advocacy program is dedicated to an effort to cease violence among teens and bullying in schools. The Blog diaries will be introduced to schools located in Contra Costa County, in an effort to improve teacher/student and parent/child relations. This program will educate youth and adults about how to express, and resolve issues. Also she will be starting a column entitled Life Honestly After, a *"Dear Aija,"* segment that will look into the questions and answers about our many life after moments.

Other written works by *Aija Butler*, include the Fiction Mystery Suspense Drama, My Nemesis a 4 part book series, "Under Lock and Key," Fiction Drama, Non-Fiction Memoirs, "Life Honestly After, The Undeniable Truth, The Fine Print, and Short Story Series, The Rebirth of My Soul, Born Again, The Resurrection," an intimate look at her walk with illness, sharing her journey through recovery and independence.

In addition to those listed above, Aija is the author of the X-files Series, Book Two Spin Cycle and Hot Tottie will be released the summer and fall of 2012, Urban Street novel, Hood Bound, will debut in August of 2012. She is the Poet/Songstress of the Poetic Experience, My Butterfly Effect debuting December 2012, and Non-Fiction Poetic Memoirs, In the Mourning and 365 Days. She is also co-author of Real or Fantasy short story collection which will hit the world of literature in June of 2012.